Sue Stratford owns and runs The Knitting Hut, a yarn and needle supplier, and she finds the yarns she stocks there and her customers a constant source of inspiration. She teaches knitting and crochet workshops as well as offering advice to customers, and loves sharing her skills with others. She always has countless knitting projects on the go. Sue lives in Milton Keynes with her husband and five children.

KNITTED
Cats
& Kittens

Dedication
This book is dedicated to my Mum, who taught me to knit and shared her passion for crafts with me, giving me a lifelong love of knitting. She also gave me my first cat. Thanks Mum x

KNITTED
Cats
& Kittens

Sue Stratford

Search Press

First published in Great Britain 2013

Search Press Limited
Wellwood, North Farm Road,
Tunbridge Wells, Kent TN2 3DR

Text copyright © Sue Stratford 2013

Photographs by Paul Bricknell at Search Press Studios

Photographs and design copyright © Search Press Ltd 2013

ISBN 978 1 84448 846 9

The Publishers and author can accept no responsibility for
any consequences arising from the information, advice or
instructions given in this publication.

Readers are permitted to reproduce any of the items in this
book for their personal use, or for the purpose of selling for
charity, free of charge and without the prior permission of
the Publishers. Any use of the items for commercial purposes
is not permitted without the prior permission of
the Publishers.

Suppliers
If you have difficulty in obtaining any of the materials and
equipment mentioned in this book, then please visit the
Search Press website for details of suppliers:
www.searchpress.com

Materials can also be obtained from the author's
own website: www.suestratford.co.uk.

Acknowledgements
I could not have written this book without the
help and support of Team Hut and my fabulous
family. Special thanks go to Babs, Claire, Heather,
Phyl, Lucy and Bekky. Also to Poppy, who gave me
her most honest opinion about each and every
cat. Thanks also to my non-knitting friends who
have put up with me knitting constantly for the
last ten months.

Printed in China

Contents

Crazy Kittens, page 14

Cosy Toes, page 34

Ginger Tom, page 37

Valentino, page 68

Monster Cat, page 72

Christmas Cat, page 94

Happy Family, page 98

Tabby Grey, page 19

Fluff Balls, page 24

Sweet Siamese, page 26

Tiny and Stripy, page 30

Rainbow, page 42

Kitty Kat, page 46

Super Cat, page 56

Clematis, page 62

Fluffy Cat, page 76

Floppy Moggy, page 80

Doorstop Cat, page 84

Alley Cat, page 89

Scratching Post, page 106

Cat Bed, page 108

Balls, page 109

Mice, page 110

Introduction

Cats come in all sorts of shapes and sizes – sleek, fluffy, skinny, plump – and all have their own special characters, which I've tried to reflect in the variety of cats I've created for this book. Just add your own imagination, change the colour or texture of the yarn you use and you will have your very own, very individual, cuddly cat.

I have really enjoyed coming up with the ideas for the playful cats and kittens in this book. Although I've included some popular breeds and types of cat – there's a sweet Siamese on page 26, a ginger tom on page 37 and a fluffy, black moggy on page 80 – this is more a book of cat 'purrsonalities' than breeds. For example, there's a delightfully cute white, fluffy cat with big blue eyes on page 76, a cheeky alley cat (page 89), and a weird but wonderful monster cat (page 72). Whatever type of cat you want to make – either for yourself or a special friend or relative – you will almost certainly find it in this book.

It's worth taking some time, before you start knitting, to look through the techniques used in the book (see page 12), as they will make your

Knit us! We'll brighten up your day!

I'm a super cat! You'll love knitting me!

cat look extra special and can make the cats easier to knit. Although I have designed the cats with children as well as adults in mind, please ensure, when attaching bells, eyes, buttons and so on, that these are stitched on firmly and cannot be pulled loose, especially by small, inquisitive hands. I have used plastic safety eyes for some of the cats. These can easily be bought on-line and one way to customise them is to paint them with metallic nail polish on the backs. This really helps the eyes shine out, especially if you are using them on a dark yarn.

Once you've knitted one of the cats or kittens in this book, you will want to make more of them, and before you know it you'll be well on the way to creating your own 'kitty universe'. So in addition to a variety of cats and kittens, I have also included patterns for some simple cat essentials: a scratching post, a cat bed, some play balls and, of course, a collection of mice.

I love all the cats and kittens in this book, and it is almost impossible to pick out a favourite, though Super Cat holds a special place in my heart. Have a careful look through all the designs in the book before deciding which one to make – some are more complicated than others – and there is bound to be one you fall madly in love with. Enjoy!

Materials

Here are just some of the yarns, threads, knitting needles and other materials and equipment I have used to make the cats in this book.

Yarns

The yarns used have been chosen with the character of each cat in mind. However, you can easily use different yarns to give your cat a completely original look. Just look at the ply or the type of yarn used (DK, Aran, laceweight and so on) and this will give you an idea of what thickness to go for. Alternatively, choose a different weight of yarn that is close to the original, but make sure you adjust the needle size used accordingly. This will prevent the shape from distorting when you stuff the cat with toy filling, and the toy filling won't show through the stitches.

The materials list for each project gives the types and colours of the yarns used. In all cases, unless the pattern states how many balls are needed, just one ball or less has been used. Quantities are only provided for projects that require more than one ball.

Knitting needles

You can use any type of knitting needle to make these cuddly characters. For the smaller projects I prefer to use double-pointed needles as they are shorter than standard needles and work well when you have relatively few stitches. Where a pattern requires stitch markers, this is stated at the beginning of the pattern.

Threads

I have used a selection of threads for embroidery and whiskers. Embroidery thread has a lovely sheen and is great for mouths and whiskers that are stitched on to the cat. For whiskers that are not stitched flat but are threaded through to give the impression of real whiskers, I have used pre-waxed linen thread, but strong sewing cotton would also work well.

Scissors

These are always an essential in any knitter's kit. Try to find a small pair to keep in your knitting bag for snipping the yarn when knitting separate arms, legs and bodies. Make sure they are nice and sharp.

Filling

All of the cats are stuffed with toy filling, which is safe for children if the cat is intended as a toy. Before you stuff your cat, tease the filling out to stop lumps forming and give an even result. Some of the cats have weighting beads in their bodies or arms and legs. For safety, sew a little cloth bag to put the beads in and stop them escaping, then put the bag of beads into the arm, leg or body before stuffing. Where weighting beads are used, they are listed at the start of the project.

Sewing needles

You will need a darning needle to sew the cats together. The size of needle used depends on the weight of the yarn – the thicker the yarn, the larger the needle you will need. Remember to pull the sewing yarn from the base near the knitting when stitching to stop the yarn stretching and breaking. Some patterns require a sewing needle for embroidery or for sewing on small eyes. Where needed, they are listed at the start of the project.

Stitch holders

Stitch holders are used in a few of the patterns to 'rest' stitches on while you continue with a different part of the cat. If you have not used them before don't worry, just slide the stitches on to the holder without twisting them and leave them there until the pattern asks you to use them again, then slide them back on to your knitting needle.

Buttons and beads

Some of the cats (and the mice) have beads as eyes. Make sure they are sewn on securely and use the appropriate size for your cat.

Safety eyes

There is a great selection of cat safety eyes to be found on-line. Different sizes and colours can make a huge difference to your finished cat. Where I have used them on darker yarns I have painted the backs of the eyes with gold or silver irridescent nail polish to make the eyes stand out and 'sparkle'. Match the colour of the polish to the eyes; for example I used gold nail polish on the amber eyes and silver on the blue and green eyes.

As an alternative to safety eyes, I have sometimes used glass eyes with a metal hook at the back to secure them. These eyes are not suitable for projects intended to be used as toys; always use safety eyes for these. Make sure the eyes are attached securely and the end of the yarn or thread used is fastened properly.

Techniques

I-cord

To make an i-cord, cast on your stitches using double-pointed needles, knit them and slide them to the other end of the same needle. Pull the yarn across the back of the needle and knit the stitches again. Repeat these instructions until the cord is long enough. By pulling the yarn behind the stitches on the needle, you close the 'gap' and give the appearance of French knitting. Alternatively, you can work the stitches in stocking stitch and sew up the seam.

Mattress stitch

This is a really neat way to join two pieces of stocking stitch together. The seam is practically invisible and not at all bulky. Begin by laying the work side by side with the right side facing you. Slip your needle through the horizontal bar between the first and second stitch of the first row on one piece and then repeat this process on the opposite piece. Work back and forth up this line of stitches for about 2.5cm (1in). Gently pull the yarn in the direction of the seam (upwards) and you will see the two sets of stitches join together. Repeat this process until you reach the top of the seam.

Wrap and turn

This technique ensures you do not end up with a 'hole' in your knitting when working short row shaping and turning your work mid-row. Slip the following stitch from the left needle to the right needle. Move the yarn from the back to the front of the work, between the needles. Slip stitch back to the right-hand needle. Turn work.

Three-needle cast off

With both pieces still on the knitting needles, place your two pieces of knitting right sides together. Using a third needle, knit the first stitch from each needle together. Now knit the next stitch from each needle together. Cast off the first stitch in the usual way by lifting it over the second stitch. Repeat until all the stitches have been cast off.

Fair Isle technique

Fair Isle is a method of knitting with two colours, in which only a few stitches in the contrasting colour are used. The yarn not being knitted is carried across the back of the work. It is best not to carry the contrasting yarn over more than two or three stitches without 'looping' the main colour around it. This will secure it to the back of the work and avoid large loops appearing.

French knots

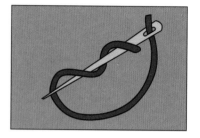

1. Bring the sewing needle through to the front of the work and wind the yarn around the needle twice.

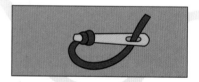

2. Take the needle through the work, half a stitch away, holding the loops around the needle with your fingers while pulling the yarn through to the back of your work.

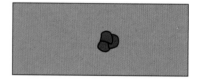

3. Pull the thread into a knot and fasten off.

Intarsia technique

Intarsia is used when knitting a block of contrasting colour. Instead of carrying the spare yarn across the back of the knitting, you work the stitches in the main colour, twist the two colours around each other (to avoid a hole forming), knit the stitches in the contrasting colour, twist again, and carry on in the main colour. This technique avoids having to carry the main colour across the back of your work.

Chain stitch

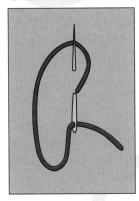 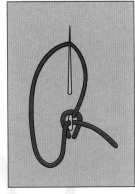 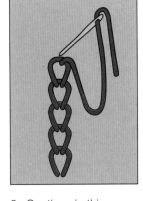

Clematis's beautifully embroidered back includes knitted leaves and flowers that have been stitched on as well as chain stitch and French knots. See page 62.

1. Bring your threaded needle from the back of the knitting to the front. Re-insert the needle from the front to the back as close as possible to the point where it first came through, forming a loop. Bring the needle point back through to the front of the knitting a short way from where it went in, so that the needle comes through inside the loop of yarn.

2. Pull the needle through the knitting and loop, remembering not to pull the loop too tightly. To continue, re-insert the needle from the front to the back and repeat the above instructions.

3. Continue in this way to create a 'chain' of stitches.

Crazy Kittens

These three mischievous kittens are knitted in sock yarn (soft yet tough, just like them!), and using the variegated variety means that no two kittens will ever be the same! The instructions for making the mice are provided on page 110, and those for the balls on page 109.

Materials

Cream 4-ply (fingering) yarn (Yarn A)
4-ply (fingering) sock yarn (Yarn B)
Toy filling
Chenille sticks
Two 4mm black beads
Pale pink 2-ply (laceweight) yarn
Strong sewing thread

Needles

2.75mm (UK 12, US 2) and 2mm (UK 14, US 0)
knitting needles
Stitch markers

Tension

7–8 sts to 2.5cm (1in) measured over SS using
2.75mm (UK 12, US 2) needles

Size

Approximately 9cm (3½in) high from front paws
to top of head

Body (and front legs)

Using Yarn A and 2.75mm (UK 12, US 2) needles,
cast on 10 sts (starting at right front foot).
Knit 1 row.
Next row: P8, turn.
K3, turn.
P3, turn.
K3, turn.
P5 (to end of row).
Next row: K2, K3B, K5.
Change to Yarn B.
Work 5 rows in SS.
Next row: K6, M1, K3, M1, K1 [12 sts].
Work 2 rows in SS.
Cast off 1 st at beg of next row (WS) [11 sts].
Cast off 5 sts at beg of next row [6 sts].
Cast on 8 sts at beg of next row [14 sts].
Cast on 1 st at beg of next row, K to last st, M1,
K1 [16 sts].
Purl 1 row.
Next row: knit to last st, M1, K1 [17 sts].
Purl 1 row.
Work 20 rows in SS, placing a marker at beg and end
of row 10.
Next row: knit to last 3 sts, K2tog, K1 [16 sts].
Purl 1 row.
Next row: cast off 1 st, knit to last 3 sts, K2tog,
K1 [14 sts].
Cast off 8 sts at beg of next row [6 sts].
Cast on 5 sts at beg of foll row (RS) [11 sts].
Cast on 1 st at beg of next row [12 sts].
Work 2 rows in SS.
Next row: K5, K2tog, K2, ssK, K1 [10 sts].

Head

Using Yarn B and 2.75mm (UK 12, US 2) needles, cast on 12 sts.

K1, M1, K5, M1, K5, M1, K1 [15 sts].

Purl 1 row.

Using the Fair Isle technique, work as follows (see page 12). Work all sts in **bold** in Yarn A and all other sts in Yarn B.

Next row: K6, M1, **K3**, M1, K6 [17 sts].

Next row: P1, M1, P6, **M1**, **P3**, **M1**, P6, M1, P1 [21 sts].

Next row: K8, **K1**, **M1**, **K3**, **M1**, **K1**, K8 [23 sts].

Next row: P1, M1, P7, **P2**, **M1**, **P3**, **M1**, **P2**, P7, M1, P1 [27 sts].

Next row: K9, **K3**, **M1**, **K3**, **M1**, **K3**, K9 [29 sts].

Next row: P9, **P11**, P9.

Next row: K9, **K11**, K9.

Next row: P9, **P11**, P9.

Next row: K9, **K2**, **K2tog**, **K3**, **ssK**, **K2**, K9 [27 sts].

Next row: P9, **P1**, **P2togtbl**, **P3**, **P2tog**, **P1**, P9 [25 sts].

Next row: K9, **K2tog**, **K3**, **ssK**, K9 [23 sts].

Next row: P8, P2togtbl, **P3**, P2tog, P8 [21 sts].

Next row: K7, K2tog, **K3**, ssK, K7 [19 sts].

Next row: P6, P2togtbl, **P3**, P2tog, P6 [17 sts].

Next row: K1, K2tog, K5, **K1**, K5, ssK, K1 [15 sts].

Work 5 rows in SS.

Change to Yarn A and knit 1 row.

Next row: P8, turn.

K3, turn.

P3, turn.

K3, turn.

P5 (to end of row).

Next row: K5, K3B, K2.

Cast off rem 10 sts.

Belly

Using Yarn A and 2.75mm (UK 12, US 2) needles, cast on 3 sts and work 2 rows in SS.

Next row: K1, M1, knit to last st, M1, K1 [5 sts].

Work 3 rows in SS.

Rep the last 4 rows twice more [9 sts].

Work 20 rows in SS.

Next row: K1, K2tog, knit to last 3 sts, ssK, K1 [7 sts].

Work 3 rows in SS.

Rep the last 4 rows once more [5 sts].

Next row: K2tog, K1, ssK [3 sts].

Thread yarn through rem sts and fasten off.

This is the last row that uses Yarn A.

Next row: P1, P2togtbl, purl to last 3 sts, P2tog, P1 [13 sts].

Cast off 3 sts, K6, cast off rem 3 sts.

With RS facing, rejoin yarn to rem 7 sts and work 12 rows in SS.

Next row: K1, K2tog, K1, ssK, K1 [5 sts].

Work 3 rows in SS.

Next row: K1, sl1, K2tog, psso, K1 [3 sts].

Purl 1 row.

Cast off.

Back leg (left)

Using Yarn A and 2.75mm (UK 12, US 2) needles, cast on 10 sts and knit 1 row.

Next row: P5, turn.

K3, turn.

P3, turn.

K3, turn.

P8 (to end of row).

Next row: K5, K3B, K2.

Change to Yarn B and work 5 rows in SS.

Next row: K4, w&t.

P3, w&t.

K3, w&t.

P3, w&t.

K3, w&t.

P4 (to end of row).

Next row: (K1, M1) twice, K3, M1, K1, M1, K4 [14 sts].

Purl 1 row.

Next row: K2, M1, K1, M1, K5, M1, K1, M1, K5 [18 sts].

Purl 1 row.

Next row: cast off 3 sts, M1, knit to last st, M1, K1 [17 sts].

Next row: cast off 6 sts, M1, purl to last st, M1, P1 [13 sts].

Work 4 rows in SS.

Next row: K1, K2tog, knit to last 3 sts, ssK, K1 [11 sts].

Next row: P1, P2togtbl, purl to last 3 sts, P2tog, P1 [9 sts].

Rep the last 2 rows once more [5 sts].

Cast off rem sts.

Back leg (right)

Using Yarn A and 2.75mm (UK 12, US 2) needles, cast on 10 sts and knit 1 row.

Next row: P8, turn.

K3, turn.

P3, turn.

K3, turn.

P5 (to end of row).

Next row: K2, K3B, K5.

Change to Yarn B and work 5 rows in SS.

Next row: K9, w&t.

P3, w&t.

K3, w&t.

P3, w&t.

K3, w&t.

P9 (to end of row).

Next row: K4, M1, K1, M1, K3, (M1, K1) twice [14 sts].

Purl 1 row.

Next row: K5, M1, K1, M1, K5, M1, K1, M1, K2 [18 sts].

Purl 1 row.

Next row: cast off 6 sts, M1, knit to last st, M1, K1 [14 sts].

Next row: cast off 3 sts, M1, purl to last st, M1, P1 [13 sts].

Work 4 rows in SS.

Next row: K1, K2tog, knit to last 3 sts, ssK, K1 [11 sts].

Next row: P1, P2togtbl, purl to last 3 sts, P2tog, P1 [9 sts].

Rep the last 2 rows once more [5 sts].

Cast off rem 5 sts.

Tail

Using Yarn B and 2.75mm (UK 12, US 2) needles, cast on 7 sts and work 4.5cm (1¾in) in SS.

Next row: K2, K2tog, K3 [6 sts].

Work 3 rows in SS.

Change to Yarn A and work 3 rows in SS.

Thread yarn through sts and fasten off.

Ears (make two)

Using Yarn B and 2.75mm (UK 12, US 2) needles, cast on 7 sts and work 2 rows in SS.

Next row: K1, K2tog, K1, ssK, K1 [5 sts].

Purl 1 row.

Next row: K2tog, K1, ssK [3 sts].

Purl 1 row.

Next row: sl1, K2tog, psso.

Fasten off rem st.

Ear linings (make two)

Using pale pink 2-ply (laceweight) yarn and 2mm (UK 14, US 0) needles, cast on 7 sts and follow instructions for ears (above).

Nose

Cast on 3 sts using a double strand of 2-ply (laceweight) yarn and 2mm (UK 14, US 0) needles.

Work 2 rows in SS.

Next row: sl1, K2tog, psso.

Fasten off rem st.

Making up

Pin the middle of the cast-off end of the cat's belly at the marker at the tail end of the body. Sew the belly to the sides of the body, being careful not to pucker the front legs by catching the WS sts at the top of each leg to the belly. Stuff with toy filling and finish sewing.

Thread a chenille stick through the front of the body and slide each end down inside one of the front legs. Gather the end of each foot into a circle by running a thread through the sts and sew the side seam of each leg. Stuff and sew the cast-off stitches of each front leg to the belly.

Sew the foot and leg seams of the back legs as for the front legs. Place a length of chenille stick inside each leg, stuff gently and sew each leg to the body, using the pictures as guidance, and sew the cast-off stitches to the belly.

Sew in the ends of the yarn on the tail, slide a length of chenille stick inside and sew it to the back of the body as shown in the pictures.

Sew the nose to the front of the head. Sew beads on to each side of the cream face marking. Pull the thread from each eye to the base of the head and tighten, pulling the eyes in. This gives the head a realistic shape. With WS together, sew the ear and ear lining together for each ear.

Sew the ears to the head using the pictures for guidance and thread strong sewing cotton through the nose to make whiskers. Sew the head to the body.

Tabby Grey

This soft and cuddly tabby will be loved by its proud owner forever! Stitch it firmly, give it a name, and this knitted kitty will bring a smile to children's faces for generations to come. The instructions for the mice and the ball are provided on pages 110 and 109 respectively.

Materials

Light grey 10-ply (Aran) yarn, 2 x 50g (2oz) balls
Dark grey 10-ply (Aran) yarn
Pink 4-ply (fingering) yarn
Two 10mm safety eyes
Black embroidery thread
Toy filling
Weighting beads

Needles

4mm (UK 8, US 6) and 2.75mm (UK 12, US 2) knitting needles

Tension

4–5 sts to 2.5cm (1in), measured over SS using 4mm (UK 8, US 6) needles

Size

Approximately 17cm (6¾in) high from front paws to top of head

Head

Made in one piece, starting at the bottom of the front of the head.
Using light grey yarn and 4mm (UK 8, US 6) needles, cast on 16 sts and work 2 rows in SS.
Next row: K1, M1, K6, M1, K2, M1, K6, M1, K1 [20 sts].
Purl 1 row.
Next row: K1, K2tog, K6, M1, K2, M1, K6, ssK, K1 [20 sts].
Purl 1 row.
Rep last 2 rows once more.
Next row: K9, M1, K2, M1, K9 [22 sts].
Purl 1 row.
Next row: K10, M1, K2, M1, K10 [24 sts].
Purl 1 row.
Next row: K11, M1, K2, M1, K11 [26 sts].

Purl 1 row.
Next row: K10, K2tog, K2, ssK, K10 [24 sts].
Next row: P9, P2togtbl, P2, P2tog, P9 [22 sts].
Next row: K8, K2tog, K2, ssK, K8 [20 sts].
Purl 1 row.
Next row: K7, K2tog, K2, ssK, K7 [18 sts].
Purl 1 row.
Next row: K1, K2tog, knit to last 3 sts, ssK, K1 [16 sts].
Next row: P1, P2togtbl, purl to last 3 sts, P2tog, P1 [14 sts].
Rep last 2 rows once more [10 sts].
Work 2 rows in SS.
This forms the top of the head.
Next row: K1, M1, knit to last st, M1, K1 [12 sts].
Next row: P1, M1, purl to last st, M1, P1 [14 sts].
Rep last 2 rows once more [18 sts].
Work 2 rows in SS.
Next row: K1, M1, knit to last st, M1, K1 [20 sts].
Work 3 rows in SS.
Next row: K1, K2tog, knit to last 3 sts, ssK, K1 [18 sts].
Purl 1 row.
Rep last 2 rows 3 more times [12 sts].
Next row: K1, K2tog, knit to last 3 sts, ssK, K1 [10 sts].
Next row: P1, P2togtbl, purl to last 3 sts, P2tog, P1 [8 sts].
Cast off.

Markings, side of head (make six)
Using dark grey yarn and 4mm (UK 8, US 6) needles, cast on 1 st and work 2 rows in SS.
Next row: Kfbf [3 sts].
Purl 1 row.
Next row: (K1, M1) twice, K1 [5 sts].
Purl 1 row.
Next row: K2tog, K1, K2tog [3 sts].
Purl 1 row.
Next row: sl1, K2tog, psso [1 st].
Fasten off rem st.

Markings, top of head (make three)
Using dark grey yarn and 4mm (UK 8, US 6) needles, cast on 1 st.
Next row: Kfbf [3 sts].
Work 3 rows in SS.
Next row: sl1, K2tog, psso.
Cast off.

Ears (make four pieces)
Using dark grey yarn and 4mm (UK 8, US 6) needles, cast on 8 sts.
Work 2 rows in SS.
Next row: K1, K2tog, knit to last 3 sts, ssK, K1 [6 sts].
Purl 1 row.
Rep last 2 rows once more [4 sts].
Next row: (K2tog) twice [2 sts].
Purl 1 row.
Next row: K2tog [1 st].
Thread yarn through rem st and fasten off.

Nose
Using pale pink yarn and 2.75mm (UK 12, US 2) needles, cast on 4 sts and work 2 rows in SS.
Next row: K2tog, ssK [2 sts].
Next row: P2tog [1 st].
Thread yarn through rem st and fasten off.

Paw pads (make four)
Using pale pink yarn and 2.75mm (UK 12, US 2) needles, cast on 3 sts and knit 1 row.
Next row: (P1, M1) twice, P1 [5 sts].
Knit 1 row.
Cast off 1 st at beg of next 2 rows [3 sts].
Purl 1 row.
Next row: sl1, K2tog, psso.
Thread yarn through rem st and fasten off.

Body
Worked in SS.
The body is worked from the back lower edge.
Using light grey yarn and 4mm (UK 8, US 6) needles, cast on 5 sts and knit 1 row.
Cast on 3 sts at beg of next 2 rows [11 sts].
Cast on 2 sts at beg of next 2 rows [15 sts].
Purl 1 row.
Break yarn, cast on 14 sts, knit across 15 body sts, turn and cast on 14 sts [43 sts].
From now on work all sts marked in **bold** using dark grey yarn and the rest of the sts in light grey yarn.
Row 1: (P2, **P3**) 3 times, P13, (**P3**, P2) 3 times.
Row 2: K1, M1, K1, (**K3**, K2) 3 times, K11, (**K3**, K2) twice, **K3**, K1, M1, K1 [45 sts].
Row 3: P3, (**P3**, P2) 3 times, P11, (**P3**, P2) 3 times, P1.
Row 4: (K4, **K1**) 3 times, K15, (**K1**, K4) 3 times.
Row 5: purl 1 row, carrying the dark grey yarn across the back of the work so it is in the right place for row 6.

Row 6: as row 4.

Row 7: as row 3.

Row 8: K1, K2tog, (**K3**, K2) 3 times, K11, (**K3**, K2) twice, **K3**, ssK, K1 [43 sts].

Row 9: as row 1.

Row 10: cast off 15 sts, K11, cast off rem 16 sts [12 sts].

Row 11: with WS facing, rejoin yarn to body sts and purl 1 row.

Row 12: K1, M1, K2, M1, K6, M1, K2, M1, K1 [16 sts].

Rows 13–31: work in SS.

Row 32: K6, K2tog, ssK, K6 [14 sts].

Row 33: purl.

You will now be shaping the front legs:

Row 34: break yarn, cast on 14 sts, K5, K2tog, ssK, K5, turn and cast on 14 sts [40 sts].

Row 35: (P2, **P3**) 3 times, P10, (**P3**, P2) 3 times.

Row 36: K1, M1, K1, (**K3**, K2) 3 times, K1, K2tog, ssK, K1, (K2, **K3**) 3 times, K1, M1, K1 [40 sts].

Row 37: P3, (**P3**, P2) 3 times, P6, (**P3**, P2) 3 times, P1.

Row 38: (K4, **K1**) 3 times, K3, K2tog, ssK, K3, (**K1**, K4) 3 times [38 sts].

Row 39: purl 1 row, carrying the dark grey yarn across the back of the work so that it is in the right place for row 40.

Row 40: (K4, **K1**) 3 times, K3, M1, K2, M1, K3, (**K1**, K4) 3 times [40 sts].

Row 41: P3, (**P3**, P2) 3 times, P6, (**P3**, P2) 3 times, P1.

Row 42: K1, K2tog, (**K3**, K2) 3 times, K1, M1, K2, M1, K3, (**K3**, K2) twice, **K3**, ssK, K1 [40 sts].

Row 43: (P2, **P3**) 3 times, P10, (**P3**, P2) 3 times.

Row 44: (K2, **K3**) 3 times, K4, M1, K2, M1, K4, (**K3**, K2) 3 times [42 sts].

Row 45: P1, M1, P1, (**P3**, P2) 3 times, P10, (**P3**, P2) twice, **P3**, P1, M1, P1 [44 sts].

Row 46: K3, (**K3**, K2) 3 times, K3, M1, K2, M1, K5, (**K3**, K2) 3 times, K1 [46 sts].

Row 47: (P4, **P1**) 3 times, P16, (**P1**, P4) 3 times.

Row 48: K22, M1, K2, M1, K22, carrying the dark grey yarn across the back of the work so that it is in the right place for row 49 [48 sts].

Row 49: (P4, **P1**) 3 times, P18, (**P1**, P4) 3 times.

Row 50: K3, (**K3**, K2) 3 times, K5, M1, K2, M1, K7, (**K3**, K2) 3 times, K1 [50 sts].

Row 51: P1, P2tog, (**P3**, P2) 3 times, P16, (**P3**, P2) twice, **P3**, P2tog, P1 [48 sts].

Row 52: (K2, **K3**) 3 times, K8, M1, K2, M1, K8, (**K3**, K2) 3 times [50 sts].

Row 53: cast off 15 sts, P18, cast off rem 16 sts [19 sts].

Row 54: with RS facing, rejoin yarn, K1, M1, K8, **K1**, K8, M1, K1 [21 sts].

Row 55: P8, **P5**, P8 [21 sts].

Row 56: K5, **K11**, K5.

Row 57: P2, **P17**, P2.

Row 58: as row 56.

Row 59: as row 55.

Row 60: K10, **K1**, K10.

Rep rows 55–60 twice more.

Row 73: as row 55.

Row 74: break yarn, cast on 14 sts, K5, **K11**, K5, turn and cast on 14 sts [49 sts].

Row 75: (P2, **P3**) 3 times, P7, **P5**, P7, (**P3**, P2) 3 times.

Row 76: K1, M1, K1, (**K3**, K2) 3 times, K6, **K3**, K7, (**K3**, K2) twice, **K3**, K1, M1, K1 [51 sts].

Row 77: P3, (**P3**, P2) 3 times, P7, **P1**, P9, (**P3**, P2) 3 times, P1.

Row 78: (K4, **K1**) 3 times, K9, **K3**, K9, (**K1**, K4) 3 times.

Row 79: P22, **P7**, P22, carrying dark grey yarn across the back of the work so that it is in the right place for row 80.

Row 80: (K4, **K1**) 3 times, K9, **K3**, K9, (**K1**, K4) 3 times.

Row 81: P3, (**P3**, P2) 3 times, P7, **P1**, P9, (**P3**, P2) 3 times, P1.

Row 82: K1, K2tog, (**K3**, K2) 3 times, K6, **K3**, K8, (**K3**, K2) twice, **K3**, ssK, K1 [49 sts].

Row 83: (P2, **P3**) 3 times, P6, **P7**, P6, (**P3**, P2) 3 times.

Row 84: cast off 22 sts, **K3**, K1, cast off 22 sts [5 sts].

Row 85: cast on 2 sts and with WS facing, P2, **P1**, P2, turn and cast on 2 sts [9 sts].

Row 86: K3, **K3**, K3.

Row 87: P1, **P7**, P1.

Row 88: as row 86.

Row 89: P4, **P1**, P4.

Rep rows 86–89 four more times.

Next row: (K1, K2tog) 3 times [6 sts].

Purl 1 row.

Next row: (K2tog) 3 times [3 sts].

Thread yarn through rem 3 sts and fasten off.

Making up

Attach the safety eyes to the front of the face, using the pictures as guidance. Sew the side seams of the head and stuff with toy filling. With wrong sides together, sew two ear pieces together. Repeat for the second ear. Place the ears on top of the head, allowing enough space between them to attach the markings. Pin three side markings on each side of the head and the three top markings between the ears. Sew the head markings in place. Using pink yarn, sew the nose in place. Embroider the mouth and whiskers using black embroidery thread.

Fold the body in half from front to back (as for Floppy Moggy, see page 82) and sew one side seam from the foot of the front leg, along the side of the body and around the back leg. Place weighting beads at the end of each paw and stuff gently with toy filling. Repeat for the other side of the body, stuffing with toy filling as you go. Sew the back seam of the body. Sew the tail seam, stuffing as you sew, and sew the base of the tail to the body.

Sew pads in place on each paw, using the picture on page 19 as guidance. Embroider three French knots (see page 12) on each paw to represent toes.

Fluff Balls

These comical cats are just about as fluffy as they get! They're quick to knit, and could be turned into brooches, key-rings or even car charms. The pattern for the scratching post is provided on page 106.

Materials
Black eyelash yarn
Black fluffy 2-ply (laceweight) yarn
Pink fluffy 2-ply (laceweight) yarn
Toy filling
6mm glass eyes

Needles
2.75mm (UK 12, US 2) and 3.25mm (UK 10, US 3) knitting needles

Tension
Not crucial, the yarn is knitted on much smaller needles than usual so this gives a tighter finish

Size
Approximately 6cm (2¼in) high

Body
Using black eyelash yarn and 3.25mm (UK 10, US 3) needles, cast on 14 sts and purl 1 row.
Work increase rows as follows:
K1, (Kfb, K1, Kfb) to last st, K1. Purl 1 row [22 sts].
K1, (Kfb, K3, Kfb) to last st, K1. Purl 1 row [30 sts].
K1, (Kfb, K5, Kfb) to last st, K1. Purl 1 row [38 sts].
K1, (Kfb, K7, Kfb) to last st, K1. Purl 1 row [46 sts].
Work 4 rows in SS.
Work decrease rows as follows:
K1, (K2tog, K7, ssK) to last st, K1. Purl 1 row [38 sts].
K1, (K2tog, K5, ssK) to last st, K1. Purl 1 row [30 sts].
K1, (K2tog, K3, ssK) to last st, K1. Purl 1 row [22 sts].
K1, (K2tog, K1, ssK) to last st, K1. Purl 1 row [14 sts].
Thread yarn through rem sts and fasten off.

Ears (make two)
Using a double strand of black 2-ply (laceweight) yarn and 2.75mm (UK 12, US 2) needles, cast on 6 sts and work 2 rows in SS.
Next row: K2tog, K2, ssK [4 sts].
Purl 1 row.
Next row: K2tog, ssK [2 sts].
Purl 1 row.
Next row: K2tog [1 st].
Thread yarn through rem st and fasten off.

Because I'm knitted in SS, the WS is 'fluffier' than the RS. This is why the WS is on the outside.

Ear lining (make two)

Using a single strand of pink 2-ply (laceweight) yarn and 2.75mm (UK 12, US 2) needles, cast on 6 sts. Follow instructions for ears.

Tail

Using eyelash yarn and 3.25mm (UK 10, US 3) needles, cast on 7 sts and work 4 rows in SS.

Next row: K1, M1, knit to last st, M1, K1 [9 sts].

Work 5 rows in SS.

Rep last 6 rows once more [11 sts].

Next row: K1, K2tog, K1, sl1, K2tog, psso, K1, K2tog, K1 [7 sts].

Thread yarn through rem sts and fasten off.

Nose

Using a double strand of pale pink 2-ply (laceweight) yarn and 2.75mm (UK 12, US 2) needles, cast on 1 st.

Row 1: Kfbf [3 sts].

Starting with a knit row, work 3 rows in SS.

Next row: sl1, K2tog, psso [1 st].

Fasten off rem st.

Making up

With WS facing outwards, sew the side seam of the fluff ball, stuff with toy filling and finish off the seam. Sew the side seam of the tail (again with WS facing outwards) but do not stuff. Attach to the back of the fluff ball.

With WS together, sew the ear linings to the ears and sew the ears to the fluff ball. Attach the eyes securely, using the picture for guidance.

Using a needle, run a length of pink yarn around the nose and gather. Sew the nose to the face of a cat. Snip away any longer lengths of yarn from around the eyes and nose if necessary so that you can see the features.

Sweet Siamese

This Siamese cat is as skinny and sleek as a knitted cat can be, but its bright blue eyes are unmistakedly Siamese. The instructions for the knitted ball are provided on page 109.

Materials
Light brown 8-ply (DK) yarn
Dark brown 8-ply (DK) yarn
Black 4-ply (fingering) yarn
Red 4-ply (fingering) yarn
Two 8mm glass eyes
Black linen thread for whiskers
Toy filling
Chenille sticks
Two 2.5cm (1in) diameter coins

Needles
3.75mm (UK 9, US 5) and 2.75mm (UK 12, US 2) knitting needles
Stitch markers

Tension
5–6 sts to 2.5cm (1in) measured over SS using 3.75mm (UK 9, US 5) needles

Size
Approximately 15cm (6in) high to top of head

Body
Using light brown yarn and 3.75mm (UK 9, US 5) knitting needles, cast on 15 sts and work 4 rows in SS.
Row 1: K6, M1, K3, M1, K6 [17 sts].
Row 2: purl (and all foll even-numbered rows).
Row 3: K7, M1, K3, M1, K7 [19 sts].
Row 5: K1, M1, K7, M1, K3, M1, K7, M1, K1 [23 sts].
Row 7: K1, M1, K9, M1, K3, M1, K9, M1, K1 [27 sts].
Row 9: K1, M1, K11, M1, K3, M1, K11, M1, K1 [31 sts].
Row 11: K1, M1, K13, M1, K3, M1, K13, M1, K1 [35 sts].
Row 13: K1, M1, K15, M1, K3, M1, K15, M1, K1 [39 sts].
Next row: K1, K2tog, knit to last 3 sts, ssK, K1 [37 sts].
Purl 1 row.
Rep the last 2 rows twice more [33 sts].
Work 2 rows in SS.
Next row: K1, K2tog, K10, K2tog, K3, ssK, K10, ssK, K1 [29 sts].
Purl 1 row.
Next row: K1, K2tog, K8, K2tog, K3, ssK, K8, ssK, K1 [25 sts].
Next row: cast off 9 sts at beg of next 2 rows [7 sts].
Work 7 rows in SS.
Cast off.

Head
Using light brown yarn and 3.75mm (UK 9, US 5) needles, cast on 8 sts.
Place markers either side of centre 2 sts.
Row 1: knit to M, M1, SM, K2, SM, M1, knit to end of row [10 sts].
Row 2: purl to M, M1, SM, P2, SM, M1, purl to end of row [12 sts].

Rep rows 1 and 2 twice more and then row 1 once more [22 sts].

Row 8: purl.

Row 9: knit to 2 sts before M, K2tog, SM, K2, SM, ssK, knit to end of row [20 sts].

Row 10: purl to 2 sts before M, P2togtbl, SM, P2, SM, P2togtbl, purl to end of row [18 sts].

Rep rows 9 and 10 once more [14 sts].

Work 2 rows in SS.

Next row: K2, K2tog, knit to last 3 sts, ssK, K1 [12 sts].

Cast off 3 sts at beg of next 2 rows [6 sts].

Work 3 rows in SS.

Next row: K1, M1, knit to last st, M1, K1 [8 sts].

Work 5 rows in SS.

Next row: K1, K2tog, knit to last 3 sts, ssK, K1 [6 sts].

Work 3 rows in SS.

Next row: K1, K2tog, ssK, K1 [4 sts].

Purl 1 row.

Please play with me!

Next row: K1, K2tog, K1 [3 sts].

Purl 1 row.

Cast off.

Face section

Using dark brown yarn and 3.75mm (UK 9, US 5) needles, cast on 6 sts. Place markers either side of the centre 2 sts.

Row 1: knit to M, M1, SM, K2, SM, M1, knit to end of row [8 sts].

Row 2: purl to M, M1, SM, P2, SM, M1, purl to end of row [10 sts].

Rep rows 1 and 2 once more and then row 1 once more [16 sts].

Purl 1 row.

Row 7: knit to 2 sts before M, K2tog, SM, K2, SM, ssK, knit to end of row [14 sts].

Row 8: purl to 2 sts before M, P2togtbl, SM, P2, SM, P2tog, purl to end of row [12 sts].

Rep rows 7 and 8 once more and then row 7 once more [6 sts].

Cast off 2 sts at beg of next 2 rows, working in SS.

Cast off rem 2 sts.

Ears (make two)

Using dark brown yarn and 3.75mm (UK 9, US 5) needles, cast on 5 sts.

Work 2 rows in SS.

Next row: K2tog, K1, ssK [3 sts].

Purl 1 row.

Next row: sl1, K2tog, psso.

Fasten off rem st.

Ear linings (make two)

Using black 4-ply (fingering) yarn and 2.75mm (UK 12, US 2) needles, cast on 5 sts.

Work 2 rows in SS.

Next row: K2tog, K1, ssK [3 sts].

Purl 1 row.

Next row: sl1, K2tog, psso.

Fasten off rem st.

Nose

Using black 4-ply (fingering) yarn and 2.75mm (UK 12, US 2) needles, cast on 4 sts.

Work 2 rows in SS.

Next row: (K2tog) twice [2 sts].

Purl 1 row.

Next row: K2tog.

Fasten off rem st.

Back leg (right)

**Using dark brown yarn and 3.75mm (UK 9, US 5) needles, cast on 6 sts and work 2 rows in SS.
Next row: K1, M1, knit to last st, M1, K1 [8 sts].
Starting with a purl row, work 9 rows in SS**.
Next row: cast off 3 sts, K1, M1, knit to last st, M1, K1 [7 sts].
Change to light brown yarn.
Next row: P1, M1, purl to last st, M1, P1 [9 sts].
Next row: K1, M1, knit to last st, M1, K1 [11 sts].
Rep last 2 rows once more [15 sts].
Work 5 rows in SS.
*Next row: K1, ssK, knit to last 3 sts, K2tog, K1*** [13 sts].
Purl 1 row*.
Rep from * to * twice more and then from * to *** once more [7 sts].
Next row: P1, P2togtbl, P1, P2tog, P1 [5 sts].
Cast off rem sts.

Back leg (left)

Follow instructions for right leg from ** to **.
Knit 1 row.
Next row: cast off 3 sts, P1, M1, purl to last st, M1, P1 [7 sts].
Change to light brown yarn.
Next row: K1, M1, knit to last st, M1, K1 [9 sts].
Next row: P1, M1, purl to last st, M1, P1 [11 sts].
Rep last 2 rows once more [15 sts].
Work 5 rows in SS.
*Next row (WS): P1, P2togtbl, purl to last 3 sts, P2tog, P1*** [13 sts].
Knit 1 row*.
Rep from * to * twice more and then from * to *** once more [7 sts].
Next row: K1, ssK, K1, K2tog, K1 [5 sts].
Cast off rem sts.

Front legs (make two)

Using dark brown yarn and 3.75mm (UK 9, US 5) needles, cast on 8 sts.
K6, turn, P4, turn, K4, turn.
P6 to end of row.
Work 12 rows in SS.
Join in light brown yarn.
K2 in light brown, K4 in dark brown, K2 in light brown.
Continuing in light brown only, cast off 2 sts at beg of next 2 rows [4 sts].
Cast off rem 4 sts.

Tail

Using dark brown yarn and 3.75mm (UK 9, US 5) needles, cast on 8 sts and work 4 rows in SS.
Next row: K1, K2tog, K2, ssK, K1 [6 sts].
Work 7cm (2¾in) in SS from increase row.
Next row: K2, K2tog, K2 [5 sts].
Work 3 rows in SS.
Next row: K1, K2tog, K2.
Purl 1 row.
Thread yarn through sts and fasten off.

Collar

Using red yarn and 2.75mm (UK 12, US 2) needles, cast on 4 sts.
Work in SS until collar is long enough to fit around cat's neck. Cast off.

Making up

Sew the head seam, stuffing firmly as you sew. The shaped part of the head is at the back. The seam will be at the front and covered by the dark brown face. Sew the head to the body, placing the cast-on edge to the neck and the two centre sts (marked while knitting) facing the front. Place the cast-on edge of the face to the base of the head (the cast-off edges form the bridge of the nose) and pin it in place using the pictures for guidance. Place a small amount of stuffing behind the face to give definition and sew it in place. Sew on the eyes.

Using the picture as a guide, sew the ears and nose in place using black yarn. Embroider the mouth and make the whiskers using black linen thread.

Sew the front seam of the body and stuff. Fold the base up and stitch it to the body, adding a little more stuffing if needed and inserting two 2.5cm (1in) diameter coins to support the cat in a sitting position. Sew the lower part of the back leg seam. Cut a piece of chenille stick to size and insert it in the lower leg. Sew the upper part of the back leg to the side of the body, adding a little stuffing to give the thigh definition. Repeat for the other leg, making sure there is an equal gap between them at the back. Sew the lower leg to the side of the cat to secure. Repeat for the second leg. Sew the front leg seams together and cut a piece of chenille stick to fit inside each leg. Sew the front legs to the body, making sure they are straight. Sew the tail side seams together and cut a piece of chenille stick to fit inside the tail. Sew the tail to the back of the body, between the back legs.

Place the collar around the cat's neck and catch the seam together.

Tiny and Stripy

This colourful duo are the perfect answer if you are looking for a knitting project that is fast, fun and frivolous! Self-patterning sock yarn works brilliantly, but any oddment of 4-ply (fingering) yarn will look great too.

Materials

Self-patterning 4-ply (fingering) sock yarn
Black sewing cotton
Small black glass beads
Toy filling

Needles

2.75mm (UK 12, US 2) double-pointed knitting needles
Stitch markers

Tension

7–8 sts to 2.5cm (1in), measured over SS in the round

Size

The large cat is approximately 6cm (2¼in) high and small one 3.5cm (1¼in) high

Big Cat

Body

Cast on 40 sts and join to work in the round.
Knit 1 round.
Next round: K10, PM, K20, PM, K10.
Next round: knit to 1 st before first M, M1, K1, SM, K1, M1, knit to 1 st before second M, M1, K1, SM, K1, M1, knit to end of round [44 sts].
Knit 2 rounds.
Rep last 3 rounds once more [48 sts].
Work 6 rounds.
Next round: knit to 3 sts before first M, K2tog, K1, SM, K1, ssK, knit to 3 sts before second M, K2tog, K1, SM, K1, ssK, knit to end of round [44 sts].
Work 3 rounds.
Rep last 4 rounds a further 3 times [32 sts].
Next round: K1, ssK, K2, K2tog, K1, SM, K1, ssK, K2, K2tog, K2, ssK, K2, K2tog, K1, SM, K1, ssK, K2, K2tog, K1 [24 sts].
Knit 1 round.
Next round: K1, ssK, K2tog, K1, SM, K1, ssK, K2tog, K2, ssK, K2tog, K1, SM, K1, K2tog, ssK, K1 [16 sts].
Knit 1 round (removing markers).
Next round: (K2tog) 8 times [8 sts].
Thread yarn through rem sts and tighten.

Our bodies are knitted in SS 'in the round' — you don't have to change to purl — you just keep knitting round and round!

Tail

Worked flat.

Cast on 8 sts and work 4 rows in SS.

*Next row: K7, w&t.

Next row: P4, w&t.

Knit to end of row.

Purl 1 row*.

Rep from * to * once more.

Next row: K1, M1, knit to last st, M1, K1 [10 sts].

Purl 1 row.

**Next row: K9, w&t.

Next row: P6, w&t.

Knit to end of row.

Purl 1 row**.

Next row: K1, M1, K to last st, M1, K1 [12 sts].

Purl 1 row.

***Next row: K11, w&t.

Next row: P8, turn.

Knit to end of row.

Purl 1 row***.

Work 4 rows in SS.

Rep from *** to *** once more.

Next row: K1, K2tog, knit to last 3 sts, ssK, K1 [10 sts].

Purl 1 row.

Rep from ** to ** once more.

Next row: (K1, K2tog) 3 times, K1 [7 sts].

Purl 1 row.

Next row: (K1, K2tog) twice, K1 [5 sts].

Next row: K2tog, K1, K2tog [3 sts].

Thread yarn through rem sts and fasten off.

Ears (make four)

Worked flat.

Cast on 6 sts and work 2 rows in SS.

Next row: K1, K2tog, ssK, K1 [4 sts].

P 1 row.

Next row: K1, K2tog, K1 [3 sts].

Next row: sl1, P2tog, psso [1 st].

Thread yarn through rem st.

Toes (make six)

Worked flat.

Cast on 1 st and work as foll:

Kfbf [3 sts].

Starting with a knit row, work 3 rows in SS.

Next row: sl1, P2tog, psso [1 st].

Thread yarn through rem st.

Feet (make two)

Worked flat.

Cast on 3 sts and work as foll:

(Kfb) 3 times [6 sts].

Starting with a knit row, work 4 rows in SS.

Next row: (K2tog) 3 times [3 sts].

Thread yarn through rem 3 sts and fasten off.

Legs (make two)

Worked flat.

Cast on 10 sts and work 6 rows in SS.

Next row: (K1, K2tog) 3 times, K1 [7 sts].

Purl 1 row.

Thread yarn through rem sts and fasten off.

Making up

Stuff the body with toy filling and sew the bottom seam, gathering each side slightly using a running stitch approximately 2.5cm (1in) up each side of the body to give it a rounded shape.

Run a length of yarn around the outside edge of each toe and gather each toe into a ball. Repeat for each foot. Sew three toes to each foot, using the picture at the top of page 32 as guidance. Sew the side seam of one leg and sew a foot to the cast-off end. Repeat for the second leg. Attach the legs to the bottom seam of the cat.

Sew the side seam of the tail, stuffing it with toy filling as you go. Attach it to the back of the body.

With WS together, sew two ear pieces together and attach them to the top of the body. Repeat for the second ear. Using a double strand of sewing cotton, sew beads in place for the eyes. Embroider the nose and mouth using the picture as guidance. Thread sewing cotton though each side of the face and trim to make whiskers.

Tiny cat

Body
Cast on 24 sts and join in the round.
Knit 1 round.
Next round: K4, PM, K12, PM, K8.
Next round: knit to 1 st before M, M1, K1, SM, K1, M1, knit to 1 st before second M, M1, K1, SM, K1, M1, knit to end of round [28 sts].
Rep last round once more [32 sts].
Knit 3 rounds.
Next round: knit to 3 sts before first M, ssK, K1, SM, K1, K2tog, knit to 3 sts before second M, ssK, K1, SM, K1, K2tog, knit to end of round [28 sts].
Work 2 rounds.
Rep last 3 rounds twice more [20 sts].
Knit 1 round.
Work from * to * [16 sts].
Knit 1 round.
Work from * to * [12 sts].
Thread yarn through rem sts and fasten off.

Ears (make two)
Worked flat.
Cast on 4 sts and knit 1 row.
Next row: P1, P2tog, P1 [3 sts].
Next row: sl1, K2tog, psso [1 st].
Fasten off rem st.

Tail
Worked flat.
Cast on 6 sts and work 4 rows in SS.
Next row: K1, M1, knit to last st, M1, K1 [8 sts].

Purl 1 row.
*K6, w&t.
P4, w&t.
Knit to end of row.
Purl 1 row*.
Rep from * to * twice more.
Next row: K2, K2tog, ssK, K2 [6 sts].
Purl 1 row.
(K2tog) 3 times [3 sts].
Purl 1 row.
Thread yarn through rem 3 sts.

Legs and feet (make two)
Cast on 6 sts.
Next row: K4, turn.
P2, turn.
K2, turn.
P2, turn.
K2, turn.
P2, turn.
Next row: K4.
Next row: purl across all sts.
Work 4 rows in SS.
Cast off.

Making up
Stuff the body with toy filling and sew the bottom seam.

Stitch the side seams of each foot together and then sew the leg seams. Attach the legs to the bottom seam of the body.

Sew the side seam of the tail, stuffing it with toy filling as you go. Attach to the back of the body.

Sew the ears in place at the top of the body with the right side at the back (this makes the ears curl forwards). Using black sewing cotton, sew beads on for eyes and embroider the nose and mouth using the picture below as guidance. Thread sewing cotton through each side of the face and trim to make whiskers.

I'm the tiniest cat in the book!

Cosy Toes

This cosy hot-water bottle cover is perfect for warming your toes on cold winter nights, and would make a loveable Christmas or birthday gift for a child or grandchild.

Materials

Fur wool, 2 x 100g (4oz) hanks
Pink 5-ply (sportweight) yarn
Two 12mm plastic safety eyes
Safety cat nose
Small hot-water bottle measuring approximately 25 x 15cm (10 x 6in)
Small amount of black yarn or embroidery thread

Needles

9mm (UK 00, US 13) and 4mm (UK 8, US 6) knitting needles

Tension

2 sts to 2.5cm (1in) measured over SS using 9mm (UK 00, US 13) needles

Size

Approximately 30cm (11¾in) in length, to top of head

Back

Using 9mm (UK 00, US 13) needles and fur wool, cast on 12 sts and work in SS until piece is long enough to fit one side of the hot-water bottle when slightly stretched. Cast off.

Front

Work as for back but work an extra 8cm (3¼in) in SS. (This will overlap at the back of the hot-water bottle to hold the bottle inside.) Cast off.

Head

Using 9mm (UK 00, US 13) needles and fur wool, cast on 3 sts.
Row 1: K1, M1, knit to last st, M1, K1 [5 sts].
Row 2: P1, M1, purl to last st, M1, P1 [7 sts].
Rep last 2 rows once more [11 sts].
Rep row 1 once more [13 sts].
Purl 1 row.
Starting with a knit row, work 3 rows in SS.
Next row: P1, P2tog, purl to last 3 sts, P2tog, P1 [11 sts].
Next row: K1, K2tog, knit to last 3 sts, ssK, K1 [9 sts].
Rep last 2 rows once more [5 sts].
Purl 1 row.
Next row: K1, M1, knit to last st, M1, K1 [7 sts].
Next row: P1, M1, purl to last st, M1, P1 [9 sts].
Rep last 2 rows once more [13 sts].
Starting with a knit row, work 3 rows in SS.
Next row: P1, P2tog, purl to last 3 sts, P2tog, P1 [11 sts].
Next row: K1, K2tog, knit to last 3 sts, ssK, K1 [9 sts].
Rep last 2 rows once more [5 sts].
Next row: P2tog, P1, P2tog [3 sts].
Cast off.

Arms (make two)

Using fur yarn and 9mm (UK 00, US 13) needles, cast on 4 sts and work 2 rows in SS.

Next row: K1, K2tog, K1 [3 sts].

Purl 1 row.

Next row: K1, Kfb, K1 [4 sts].

Work 2 rows in SS.

Cast off.

Feet (make two)

Using fur yarn and 9mm (UK 00, US 13) needles, cast on 4 sts and knit 1 row.

Next row: P1, M1, purl to last st, M1, P1 [6 sts].

Work 4 rows in SS.

Next row: K2tog, K2, K2tog [4 sts].

Purl 1 row.

Cast off.

Tail

Using fur yarn and 9mm (UK 00, US 13) needles, cast on 8 sts and work 4 rows in SS.

Row 1: K5, w&t.

Row 2: P2, w&t.

Row 3: K2, w&t.

Row 4: P2, w&t.

Row 5: knit to end of row.

Row 6: purl.

Rep rows 1–6 twice more.

Work 3 rows in SS.

Next row: (P2tog) 4 times [4 sts].

Thread yarn through sts and fasten off.

Ears (make two)

Worked in GS.

Using fur yarn and 9mm (UK 00, US 13) needles, cast on 4 sts and knit 2 rows.

Next row: (K2tog) twice [2 sts].

Thread yarn through rem sts and tighten.

Bow

Using pink yarn and 4mm (UK 8, US 6) needles, cast on 10 sts and knit until work measures 15cm (6in).

Cast off.

Centre of bow

Using pink yarn and 4mm (UK 8, US 6) needles, cast on 5 sts and work 5cm (2in) in GS.

Cast off.

Ribbon ends (make two)

Using pink yarn and 4mm (UK 8, US 6) needles, cast on 10 sts and work 3cm (1¼in) in GS.

Next row: K1, K2tog, knit to end of row [9 sts].

Knit 1 row.

Rep last 2 rows a further 7 times until 2 sts rem.

Next row: K2tog.

Fasten off rem st.

Making up

Fold the head in half with the wrong sides facing outwards. The cast-on and cast-off edges form the neck edge. Fit the safety eyes and nose in place and sew the side seams. With black thread, embroider the mouth and whiskers. Pin the body front and back together with the wrong sides facing outwards and pin the head in place. Sew the side seams of the body and sew the head to the top of the body. The top of the hot-water bottle will fit into the head. Sew the ears to the top of the head. Fold the flap from the front of the cover to the back and sew it neatly to the side seams. Fold the tail together, wrong sides outwards, and sew the seam. Attach it to the seam on the side of the cat. Fold the foot in half and sew the seams. Repeat for the second foot. Sew the feet to the base of the cover. Repeat for the arms, but sew them to the side seams using the picture as guidance.

Make the bow by folding the main part of the bow in half lengthways and sewing it together at the back. Place the centre of the bow around the middle, tightening it to make the bow look tied. Sew it in place. Sew each ribbon in place behind the bow at an angle, using the picture for guidance.

Ginger Tom

This cat's really got the cream – too much, perhaps, but though he's a little over-weight he's very cuddly, and his squashy belly means he is as comfortable sitting up as he is lying down. You'll just love this gorgeous ginger tom!

Materials

Cream 5-ply (sportweight) yarn
Orange 5-ply (sportweight) yarn
Small amount of pink 4-ply (fingering) yarn
Two 8mm plastic safety eyes, painted on the backs with silver nail polish
Small amount of black embroidery thread
Toy filling
Weighting beads

Needles

3.25mm (UK 10, US 3) and 2.75mm (UK 12, US 2) knitting needles
Two stitch markers

Tension

6 sts per 2.5cm (1in) measured over SS using 5-ply (sportweight) yarn and 3.25mm (UK 10, US 3) needles

Size

Approximately 19cm (7½in) tall, from paws to top of head

Body back

Using cream yarn and 3.25mm (UK 10, US 3) needles, cast on 12 sts and work 4 rows in SS.
Row 1: K1, K2tog, knit to last 3 sts, ssK, K1 [10 sts].
Row 2: purl.
Rep row 1 once more [8 sts].
Next row: P1, P2tog, purl to last 3 sts, P2togtbl, P1 [6 sts].
Next row: K6, pick up 5 sts knitwise and knit these sts along decreased edge [11 sts].

Next row: P11, pick up and purl 5 sts purlwise and purl these sts along decreased edge [16 sts].

Next row: K1, M1, knit to last st, M1, K1 [18 sts].

Next row: P1, M1, purl to last st, M1, P1 [20 sts].

Rep last 2 rows once more [24 sts].

Join in orange yarn and from now on work all sts in **bold** using orange yarn and all other sts using cream yarn. Use the Fair Isle technique to carry the yarn at the back of the work (see page 12).

NB: wind off the orange yarn to work the markings on either side to avoid carrying the yarn right across the back of the work.

Row 1: **K2**, K20, **K2**.

Row 2: **P4**, P16, **P4**.

Row 3: **K7**, K10, **K7**.

Row 4: as row 2.

Row 5: as row 1.

Row 6: purl all sts.

Rep last 6 rows once more.

Row 13: as row 1.

Row 14: as row 2.

Row 15: **K7**, K1, K2tog, K4, ssK, K1, **K7** [22 sts].

Row 16: **P4**, P14, **P4**.

The next row is the last one to use orange yarn.

Row 17: **K2**, K6, K2tog, K2, ssK, K6, **K2** [20 sts].

Row 18: purl all sts.

Row 19: K1, K2tog, K5, K2tog, ssK, K5, ssK, K1 [16 sts].

Row 20: purl all sts.

Row 21: K1, K2tog, K4, K2tog, K4, ssK, K1 [13 sts].

Row 22: purl all sts.

Row 23: K1, K2tog, knit to last 3 sts, ssK, K1 [11 sts].

Row 24: purl all sts.

Row 25: as row 23 [9 sts].

Row 26: purl all sts.

Cast off rem 9 sts.

Body front

Using cream yarn and 3.25mm (UK 10, US 3) needles, cast on 8 sts and purl 1 row.

Row 1: K1, M1, (K2, M1) 3 times, K1 [12 sts].

Row 2: purl 1 row.

Row 3: K1, M1, K3, M1, K4, M1, K3, M1, K1 [16 sts].

Row 4: purl 1 row.

Row 5: K1, M1, K4, M1, K6, M1, K4, M1, K1 [20 sts].

Row 6: purl 1 row.

Row 7: K1, M1, K5, M1, K8, M1, K5, M1, K1 [24 sts].

Row 8: purl 1 row.

Row 9: K1, M1, K6, M1, K10, M1, K6, M1, K1 [28 sts].

Join in orange yarn and work as follows, using the Fair Isle technique (see page 12) to carry the yarn at the back of the work.

Row 10: **P2**, P24, **P2**.

Row 11: **K4**, K20, **K4**.

Row 12: **P7**, P14, **P7**.

Row 13: as row 11.

Row 14: as row 10.

Row 15: knit 1 row.

Rep rows 10–15 once more.

Row 22: **P2**, P24, **P2**.

Row 23: **K4**, K4, K2tog, K8, ssK, K4, **K4** [26 sts].

Row 24: **P7**, P12, **P7**.

Row 25: **K4**, K4, K2tog, K6, ssK, K4, **K4** [24 sts].

The next row is the last to use orange yarn.

Row 26: **P2**, P20, **P2**.

Row 27: K8, K2tog, K4, ssK, K8 [22 sts].

Row 28: purl all sts.

Row 29: K1, K2tog, K5, K2tog, K2, ssK, K5, ssK, K1 [18 sts].

Row 30: purl all sts.

Row 31: K1, K2tog, K4, K2tog, ssK, K4, ssK, K1 [14 sts].

Row 32: P1, P2tog, purl to last 3 sts, P2togtbl, P1 [12 sts].

Row 33: K1, K2tog, K2, K2tog, K2, ssK, K1 [9 sts].

Row 34: P1, P2tog, P3, P2togtbl, P1 [7 sts].

Cast off rem 7 sts.

Head

Made in one piece starting from the lower front edge.

Using cream yarn and 3.25mm (UK 10, US 3) needles, cast on 9 sts.

Row 1: knit all sts.

Row 2: P1, M1, purl to last st, M1, P1 [11 sts].

Using the Fair Isle technique to carry the yarn (see page 12), work as follows. Work all sts in **bold** in orange and all other sts in cream.

Row 3: **K1**, M1, knit to last st, M1, **K1** [13 sts].

Row 4: **P1**, **M1**, **P3**, P1, M1, P3, M1, P1, **P3**, **M1**, **P1** [17 sts].

Row 5: **K3**, K4, M1, K3, M1, K4, **K3** [19 sts].

Row 6: P8, M1, P3, M1, P8 [21 sts].

Row 7: **K2**, K7, M1, K3, M1, K7, **K2** [23 sts].

Row 8: **P3**, P17, **P3**.

Row 9: **K2**, K19, **K2**.

Row 10: purl all sts.

Row 32: **P1**, **P2tog**, P7, **P2togtbl**, **P1** [11 sts].
Row 33: knit all sts.
Row 34: purl all sts.
Cast off.

Arms (make two)

Using cream yarn and 3.25mm (UK 10, US 3) needles, cast on 12 sts.

Row 1: knit all sts.

Using the Fair Isle technique to carry the yarn (see page 12), work as follows. Work all sts in **bold** in orange and all other sts in cream.

Row 2: **P2**, (P3, **P2**) twice.

Row 3: **K3**, K1, **K4**, K1, **K3**.

Row 4: as row 2.

Rep rows 1–4 once more.

Work 2 rows in SS.

Next row: K1, M1, K4, M1, K2, M1, K4, M1, K1 [16 sts].

Starting with a purl row, work 3 rows in SS.

Next row: K1, K2tog, K2, ssK, K2, K2tog, K2, ssK, K1 [12 sts].

Cast off on WS.

Feet (make two)

Using cream yarn and 3.25mm (UK 10, US 3) needles, cast on 6 sts and knit 1 row.

Next row: P1, M1, purl to last st, M1, P1 [8 sts].

Next row: K1, M1, knit to last st, M1, K1 [10 sts].

Work 5 rows in SS.

Next row: K1, K2tog, knit to last 3 sts, ssK, K1 [8 sts].

Purl 1 row.

Next row: K1, M1, knit to last st, M1, K1 [10 sts].

Work 5 rows in SS.

Next row: K1, K2tog, knit to last 3 sts, ssK, K1 [8 sts].

Next row: P1, P2togtbl, purl to last 3 sts, P2tog, P1 [6 sts].

Knit 1 row.

Cast off on WS.

Legs (make two)

Using cream yarn and 3.25mm (UK 10, US 3) needles, cast on 14 sts.

Row 1: knit all sts.

Row 2: purl all sts.

Using the Fair Isle technique to carry the yarn (see page 12), work as follows. Work all sts in **bold** in orange and all other sts in cream.

Row 3: **K2**, (K4, **K2**) twice.

Row 4: **P3**, P2, **P4**, P2, **P3**.

Row 11: **K2**, K7, K2tog, K1, ssK, K7, **K2** [21 sts].
Row 12: **P4**, P4, P2tog, P1, P2togtbl, P4, **P4** [19 sts].
Row 13: **K2**, K5, K2tog, K1, ssK, K5, **K2** [17 sts].
Row 14: purl all sts.
Row 15: K1, K2tog, K3, **K1**, K3, **K1**, K3, ssK, K1 [15 sts].
Row 16: P1, P2tog, P2, **P1**, P3, **P1**, P2, P2togtbl, P1 [13 sts].
Row 17: K1, K2tog, **K3**, K1, **K3**, ssK, K1 [11 sts].
Row 18: P2, **P3**, P1, **P3**, P2.
Row 19: K1, M1, K1, **K3**, K1, **K3**, K1, M1, K1 [13 sts].
Row 20: P1, M1, P3, **P1**, P3, **P1**, P3, M1, P1 [15 sts].
Row 21: **K2**, K3, **K1**, K3, **K1**, K3, **K2** [15 sts].
Row 22: **P4**, P7, **P4**.
Row 23: **K2**, K11, **K2**.
Row 24: purl all sts.
Row 25: as row 23.
Row 26: **P3**, P9, **P3**.
Row 27: as row 23.
Row 28: purl all sts.
Row 29: **K3**, K9, **K3**.
Row 30: as row 22.
Row 31: **K1**, **K2tog**, K9, **ssK**, **K1** [13 sts].

Row 5: as row 3.
Row 6: as row 2.
Row 7: as row 1.
Row 8: **P2**, (P4, **P2**) twice.
Row 9: **K3**, K2, **K4**, K2, **K3**.
Row 10: as row 8.
Row 11: knit all sts.
Row 12: purl all sts.
Cast off.

Tail

Using cream yarn and 3.25mm (UK 10, US 3) needles, cast on 12 sts and work 4 rows in SS.

Using the Fair Isle technique to carry the yarn (see page 12), work as follows. Work all sts in **bold** in orange and all other sts in cream.

Row 1: **K2**, (K3, **K2**) twice.
Row 2: **P3**, P1, **P4**, P1, **P3**.
Row 3: as row 1.
Row 4: purl all sts.
Row 5: knit all sts.
Row 6: purl all sts.
Rep last 6 rows twice more.
Next row: (K1, K2tog) 4 times [8 sts].

Purl 1 row.
Next row: (K2tog) 4 times.
Thread yarn through rem 4 sts and fasten off.

Ears (make four)

Using orange yarn and 3.25mm (UK 10, US 3) needles, cast on 7 sts and work 2 rows in SS.
Next row: K2tog, knit to last 2 sts, ssK [5 sts].
Purl 1 row.
Rep last 2 rows once more.
Next row: sl1, K2tog, psso.
Fasten off rem st.

Nose

Using pink yarn and 2.75mm (UK 12, US 2) needles, cast on 5 sts and work 2 rows in SS.
Next row: K2tog, K1, ssK [3 sts].
Purl 1 row.
Next row: sl1, K2tog, psso.
Fasten off rem st.

Making up

Sew the side seams of the arms and cast-off edges of the paws together, matching the orange markings. Stuff with toy filling and oversew two stitches on to the paws in orange yarn to give the appearance of pads. Sew each of the feet together, stuffing with toy filling as you go, and oversew two stitches as for the paws on the arms. Sew the side seam of each leg and stuff the legs with toy filling. Sew the bottom of one leg to the top of a foot and repeat for the second leg and foot.

Pin the back and front of the body together, pinning the arms and legs in place into the seam. Sew the seam of the body. Place weighting beads at the bottom of the body and stuff with toy filling, sewing the arms and legs in place as you go.

Attach safety eyes to the head, sew the seam and stuff with toy filling. With WS together, sew two ear pieces together. Repeat for the second ear and sew the ears to the top of the head, placing them over the seam and using the picture as guidance. Sew the nose in place. Stitch the mouth and whiskers in place using black embroidery thread. Using a needle and thread, sew from the base of the head to the back of each eye, pull the thread back down to the base and tighten. This gives a fantastic shape to the head.

Sew the head to the body. Sew the side seam of the tail, matching the orange markings, and stuff with toy filling. Sew the tail to the back of the cat using the picture as guidance.

Rainbow

They say a leopard never changes its spots, but cats can definitely change their stripes! This zany cat is soaking up the the sunshine, but try knitting him in blues and purples for a more dreamy night-time mood.

Materials

Orange 5-ply (sportweight) yarn
Yellow 5-ply (sportweight) yarn
Green 5-ply (sportweight) yarn
Turquoise 5-ply (sportweight) yarn
Black 4-ply (fingering) yarn
Two black plastic 8mm safety eyes
Toy filling
Small piece of heavy-weight interfacing or card cut to fit inside the base

Needles

3.25mm (UK 10, US 3) and 2.75mm (UK 12, US 2) knitting needles

Tension

6 sts to 2.5cm (1in) measured over GS using 3.25mm (UK 10, US 3) needles

Size

Approximately 32cm (12½in) tall, from paws to top of head

Stripe pattern

Each piece of the cat is knitted in a GS two-row stripe pattern which is as follows:
Knit 2 rows in orange.
Knit 2 rows in yellow.
Knit 2 rows in green.
Knit 2 rows in turquoise.

Head

NB: count the cast-on row as the first row of the stripe pattern.

Using orange yarn and 3.25mm (UK 10, US 3) needles, cast on 30 sts and work as follows, keeping to the stripe pattern above.

Next row: K7, M1, K1, M1, K6, M1, K2, M1, K6, M1, K1, M1, K7 [36 sts].
Knit 1 row.
Next row: K8, M1, K1, K2tog, K6, M1, K2, M1, K6, ssK, K1, M1, K8 [38 sts].
Knit 1 row.
Next row: K9, M1, K1, K2tog, K6, M1, K2, M1, K6, ssK, K1, M1, K9 [40 sts].
Knit 1 row.
Next row: K10, M1, K1, K2tog, K6, M1, K2, M1, K6, ssK, K1, M1, K10 [42 sts].
Knit 1 row.
Next row: K20, M1, K2, M1, K20 [44 sts].
Knit 1 row.
Next row: K21, M1, K2, M1, K21 [46 sts].
Knit 1 row.

Knit 1 row.

Rep last 2 rows twice more [14 sts].

Work 2 rows in GS.

Next row: keeping stripe pattern correct, cast on 21 sts at beg of row, knit across 35 sts on needle, turn and cast on 21 sts [56 sts].

Knit 23 rows in stripe pattern.

Change colour and knit 1 row.

Next row: K2, K2tog, (K5, K2tog) 7 times, K3 [48 sts].

Work 6 rows in stripe pattern.

Change colour and knit 1 row.

Next row: K2, K2tog, (K4, K2tog) 7 times, K2 [40 sts].

Work 6 rows in stripe pattern.

Change colour and knit 1 row.

Next row: K1, K2tog, (K3, K2tog) 7 times, K2 [32 sts].

Work 4 rows in stripe pattern.

Change colour and knit 1 row.

Next row: K1, K2tog, (K2, K2tog) 7 times, K1 [24 sts].

Work 2 rows in GS.

Change colour and knit 1 row.

Next row: (K1, K2tog) 8 times [16 sts].

Thread yarn through rem sts and secure.

Legs (make two)

Using orange yarn and 3.25mm (UK 10, US 3) needles, cast on 16 sts and work 7 repeats of the two-row stripe pattern. Cast off.

Foot (make two)

Work in stripe pattern.

Using orange yarn and 3.25mm (UK 10, US 3) needles, cast on 7 sts and knit 1 row.

Next row: K1, M1, knit to last st, M1, K1 [9 sts].

Next row: K1, M1, knit to last st, M1, K1 [11 sts].

Knit 5 rows.

Row 1: K1, M1, knit to last st, M1, K1 [13 sts].

Row 2: knit 1 row.

Rep last 2 rows once more [15 sts].

Knit 2 rows.

Row 1: K1, K2tog, knit to last 3 sts, ssK, K1 [13 sts].

Rep last row once more [11 sts].

Knit 2 rows.

Next row: K1, M1, knit to last st, M1, K1 [13 sts].

Rep last row once more [15 sts].

Knit 2 rows.

Row 1: K1, K2tog, knit to last 3 sts, ssK, K1 [13 sts].

Row 2: knit.

Rep last 2 rows once more [11 sts].

Work 4 rows in SS.

Next row: K22, M1, K2, M1, K22 [48 sts].

Knit 1 row.

Next row: K21, K2tog, K2, ssK, K21 [46 sts].

Next row: K20, K2tog, K2, ssK, K20 [44 sts].

Knit 1 row.

Next row: K19, K2tog, K2, ssK, K19 [42 sts].

Knit 1 row.

Next row: K18, K2tog, K2, ssK, K18 [40 sts].

Knit 1 row.

Next row: K17, K2tog, K2, ssK, K17 [38 sts].

Knit 1 row.

Next row: K1, K2tog, knit to last 3 sts, ssK, K1 [36 sts].

Rep this row twice more [32 sts].

Next row: K6, K2tog, ssK, K12, ssK, K2tog, K6 [28 sts].

Next row: K5, K2tog, ssK, K10, ssK, K2tog, K5 [24 sts].

Next row: K4, K2tog, ssK, K8, ssK, K2tog, K4 [20 sts].

Next row: K3, K2tog, ssK, K6, ssK, K2tog, K3 [16 sts].

Cast off.

Body

Worked in two-row stripe pattern.

Using orange yarn and 3.25mm (UK 10, US 3) needles, cast on 14 sts and work 3 rows in GS.

Next row: K1, M1, knit to last st, M1, K1 [16 sts].

Knit 1 row.

Rep last 2 rows twice more [20 sts].

Work 14 rows in stripe pattern.

Next row: K1, K2tog, knit to last 3 sts, ssK, K1 [18 sts].

Next row: K1, K2tog, knit to last 3 sts, ssK, K1 [9 sts].
Next row: K1, K2tog, knit to last 3 sts, ssK, K1 [7 sts].
Cast off.

Arms (make two)

Using orange yarn and 3.25mm (UK 10, US 3) needles, cast on 14 sts and work 5 repeats of the two-row stripe pattern. Work paw in stripe pattern.
Next row: K1, M1, K5, M1, K2, M1, K5, M1, K1 [18 sts].
Knit 1 row.
Next row: K1, M1, K7, M1, K2, M1, K7, M1, K1 [22 sts].
Knit 3 rows.
Next row: K1, K2tog, K5, ssK, K2, K2tog, K5, ssK, K1 [18 sts].
Next row: K1, K2tog, K3, ssK, K2, K2tog, K3, ssK, K1 [14 sts].
Cast off.

Tail

Using orange yarn and 3.25mm (UK 10, US 3) needles, cast on 14 sts and work 9 repeats of the two-row stripe pattern.
Knit 4 rows in stripe pattern.
Next row: (K2, K2tog) 3 times, K2 [11 sts].
Knit 1 row.
Next row: K1, (K2tog) 5 times [6 sts].
Thread yarn through rem sts and fasten off.

Nose

Using black yarn and 2.75mm (UK 12, US 2) needles, cast on 5 sts and work 2 rows in SS.
Next row: K2tog, K1, K2tog [3 sts].
Purl 1 row.
Next row: sl1, K2tog, psso [1 st].
Fasten off rem st.

Ears (make four)

(Worked in stripe pattern throughout.)
Using orange yarn and 3.25mm (UK 10, US 3) needles, cast on 8 sts and knit 2 rows in stripe pattern.
Next row: K1, K2tog, knit to last 3 sts, ssK, K1 [6 sts].
Knit 1 row.
Rep last 2 rows once more [4 sts].
Next row: (K2tog) twice [2 sts].
Next row: K2tog.
Fasten off rem st.

Making up

Use the orange yarn to sew the cat together as each part of the cat starts with orange yarn.

Sew the back seam and cast-off edge of the head. Attach the safety eyes, using the picture for guidance. Stuff the head, gather the cast-on edge, and secure. Place two ears WS together, and carefully sew them together using the ends of the appropriate colour yarns. Repeat for the second ear and sew the ears into place. Sew the nose in place and embroider the mouth and whiskers.

Sew the back seam of the body, fold up the base and sew it in place. Lay a piece of heavyweight interfacing or card in the base to make it firm and flat. Stuff with toy filling, gather the neck-edge seam and sew closed. Sew the head to the body. Sew the seams of the arms and paws. Stuff with toy filling. Using orange yarn, oversew the ends using the picture as guidance to give the appearance of paws. Sew the arms to the side of the body. Sew the foot seams and stuff with toy filling. Using orange yarn, oversew to make the paws (use the picture for guidance). Sew one of the leg seams and stuff with toy filling. Sew the bottom of the leg to the top of the foot. Repeat for the second foot and leg. Sew the legs in place. Sew the tail seam and stuff with toy filling. Sew to the back of the body.

Kitty Kat

A girl just can't have too many clothes – and that goes for cats too. This fabulous feline has an outfit for bedtime and one for daytime, and just loves to dress up.

Materials

Grey 8-ply (DK) yarn
Cream 8-ply (DK) yarn
Small amount of pink 2-ply (laceweight) yarn
Two 9mm plastic safety eyes, painted on the back with silver nail polish
Small amount of black embroidery thread
Toy filling

Needles

3.75mm (UK 9, US 5) knitting needles
Two stitch markers

Tension

4–5 sts to 2.5cm (1in) measured over SS

Size

Approximately 25cm (9¾in) tall, from paws to top of head

Body back

Using grey yarn, cast on 10 sts and work 2 rows in SS.
Row 1: K1, M1, knit to last st, M1, K1 [12 sts].
Row 2: P1, M1, purl to last st, M1, P1 [14 sts].
Rep last 2 rows once more [18 sts].
Rep row 1 once more [20 sts].
Work 7 rows in SS.
Next row: K1, K2tog, knit to last 3 sts, ssK, K1 [18 sts].
Purl 1 row.
Rep last 2 rows twice more [14 sts].
Next row: K1, K2tog, knit to last 3 sts, ssK, K1 [12 sts].
Work 3 rows in SS.
Rep last 4 rows twice more [8 sts].
Cast off.

Body front

Using grey yarn, cast on 10 sts and work 2 rows in SS.

Place markers 4 sts in from each end.

Row 1: K1, M1, knit to M, SM, M1, knit to M, M1, SM, knit to last st, M1, K1 [14 sts].

Row 2: P1, M1, purl to last st, M1, P1 [16 sts].

Rep last 2 rows twice more [28 sts].

Rep row 1 once more [32 sts].

Starting with a purl row work 7 rows in SS.

Next row: K1, K2tog, knit to M, SM, K2tog, knit to 2 sts before M, ssK, SM, knit to last 3 sts, ssK, K1 [28 sts].

Purl 1 row.

Rep last 2 rows 3 more times [16 sts].

Remove markers.

Next row: K1, K2tog, knit to last 3 sts, ssK, K1 [14 sts].

Work 3 rows in SS.

Rep last 4 rows once more [12 sts].

Next row: K1, K2tog, knit to last 3 sts, ssK, K1 [10 sts].

Purl 1 row.

Cast off.

Head

Using grey yarn, cast on 12 sts.

Next row: K1, M1, K5, M1, K5, M1, K1 [15 sts].

Purl 1 row.

Using the Fair Isle technique to carry the yarn, work as follows (see page 12). Work all sts in **bold** in cream and all other sts in grey.

Next row: K6, M1, **K3**, M1, K6 [17 sts].

Next row: P1, M1, P6, **M1**, **P3**, **M1**, P6, M1, P1 [21 sts].

Next row: K8, **K1**, **M1**, **K3**, **M1**, **K1**, K8 [23 sts].

Next row: P1, M1, P7, **P2**, **M1**, **P3**, **M1**, **P2**, P7, M1, P1 [27 sts].

Next row: K9, **K3**, **M1**, **K3**, **M1**, **K3**, K9 [29 sts].

Next row: P9, **P11**, P9.

Next row: K9, **K11**, K9.

Next row: P9, **P11**, P9.

Next row: K9, **K2**, **K2tog**, **K3**, **SSK**, **K2**, K9 [27 sts].

Next row: P9, **P1**, **P2togtbl**, **P3**, **P2tog**, **P1**, P9 [25 sts].

Next row: K9, **K2tog**, **K3**, **ssK**, K9 [23 sts].

Next row: P8, P2togtbl, **P3**, P2tog, P8 [21 sts].

Next row: K7, K2tog, **K3**, ssK, K7 [19 sts].

Next row: P6, P2togtbl, **P3**, P2tog, P6 [17 sts].

Next row: K1, K2tog, K5, **K1**, K5, ssK, K1 [15 sts].

This is the last row that uses cream yarn.

Next row: P1, P2togtbl, purl to last 3 sts, P2tog, P1 [13 sts].

Cast off 3 sts, K6, cast off rem 3 sts.

With WS facing, rejoin yarn to rem 7 sts and work 10 rows in SS.

Next row: P1, P2togtbl, K1, P2tog, P1 [5 sts].

Work 2 rows in SS.

Next row: K1, sl1, K2tog, psso, K1 [3 sts].

Purl 1 row.

Cast off.

Nose

Using a double strand of pink laceweight yarn, cast on 5 sts and work 2 rows in SS.

Next row: K2tog, K1, ssK [3 sts].

Purl 1 row.

Next row: sl1, K2tog, psso.

Fasten off rem st.

Arms (make two)

Using grey, cast on 10 sts and work 10 rows in SS.

Change to cream yarn and work 2 rows in SS.

Next row: K1, M1, K3, M1, K2, M1, K3, M1, K1 [14 sts].

Purl 1 row.

Next row: K1, M1, K5, M1, K2, M1, K5, M1, K1 [18 sts].

Purl 1 row.

Next row: K1, K2tog, K3, ssK, K2, K2tog, K3, ssK, K1 [14 sts].

Cast off on WS.

Feet (make two)

Using cream yarn, cast on 6 sts and knit 1 row.

Next row: P1, M1, purl to last st, M1, P1 [8 sts].

Next row: K1, M1, knit to last st, M1, K1 [10 sts].

Work 5 rows in SS.

Next row: K1, K2tog, knit to last 3 sts, ssK, K1 [8 sts].

Purl 1 row.

Next row: K1, M1, knit to last st, M1, K1 [10 sts].

Work 5 rows in SS.

Next row: K1, K2tog, knit to last 3 sts, ssK, K1 [8 sts].

Next row: P1, P2togtbl, purl to last 3 sts, P2tog, P1 [6 sts].

Knit 1 row.

Cast off on WS.

Legs (make two)

Using grey yarn, cast on 10 sts and work 12 rows in SS.

Cast off.

Tail

Using grey yarn, cast on 9 sts and work 10 rows in SS.

*Next row: K6, w&t.

Next row: P3, w&t.

Knit to end of row.

Purl 1 row.

Rep from * twice more.

Work 11 rows in SS.

Change to cream yarn and purl 1 row.

Next row: (K1, K2tog) 3 times [6 sts].

Purl 1 row.

Next row: (K2tog) 3 times [3 sts].

Thread yarn through rem sts and tighten.

Ears (make four)

Using grey yarn, cast on 7 sts and work 2 rows in SS.

Next row: K2tog, knit to last 2 sts, ssK [5 sts].

Purl 1 row.

Rep last 2 rows once more [3 sts].

Next row: sl1, K2tog, psso.

Fasten off rem st.

Making up

Sew the body side seams, stuffing with toy filling as you go. Attach the safety eyes to the head and sew the gusset into place at the back of the head. Stuff with toy filling. With wrong sides together, sew two ear pieces together. Repeat for the second ear and sew the ears to the top of the head, using the picture as guidance. Sew the nose in place. Using black embroidery thread, embroider the mouth. Stitch the whiskers in place. Using a needle and thread, sew from the base of the head to the back of each eye, pull the thread back down to the base and tighten. This gives a fantastic shape to the head.

Sew the head to the body. Sew the side seams of the arms and the cast-off edges of the paws together. Stuff with toy filling and oversew two stitches on to the paws in cream yarn to give the appearance of paws.

Sew each foot together, stuffing with toy filling as you go. Oversew two stitches on to each foot as for the paws on the arms. Sew the side seam of each leg and stuff with toy filling. Join one of the legs to a foot and sew the other end of the leg to the bottom seam of the body. Repeat for the second leg.

Sew the side seam of the tail, stuff with toy filling and sew to the back of the cat using the picture as guidance.

Kitty Kat's daytime clothes

Materials

Orange 5-ply (sportweight) yarn
Blue 5-ply (sportweight) yarn
Two buttons for dress with fish motifs
Two small buttons for shoes
Small amount of narrow ribbon

Needles

3.25mm (UK 10, US 3) and 2.75mm
(UK 12, US 2) knitting needles

Tension

Approximately 6 sts to 2.5cm (1in) measured
over SS using 3.25mm (UK 10, US 3) needles

Bloomers

Made in two halves.

Using orange yarn and 2.75mm (UK 12, US 2)
needles, cast on a picot edge as follows:

(Cast on 5 sts, cast off 2 sts, pass st on RH needle to
LH needle) 8 times, cast on 2 sts [26 sts].

Next row: (K3, inc 1 (by picking up the loop laying
before the next st and knitting into it)), rep to last 2
sts, K2 [34 sts].

Purl 1 row.

Next row: (K2tog) 17 times [17 sts].

Purl 1 row.

Change to 3.25mm (UK 10, US 3) needles.

Next row: (Kfb) 17 times [34 sts].

Purl 1 row.

Next row: cast off 3 sts, M1, (K2, M1) 13 times,
K4 [45 sts].

Next row: cast off 3 sts, purl to end of row [42 sts].

Next row: K1, K2tog, K6, (M1, K5) to last 8 sts, M1,
K5, ssK, K1 [46 sts].

Next row: P1, P2togtbl, purl to last 3 sts, P2tog,
P1 [44 sts].

Work 14 rows in SS.

Next row: (K2, K2tog) 11 times [33 sts].

Purl 1 row.

Work 3 rows in (K1, P1) rib.

Next row: (WS) (rib 4 sts, P2tog, yo) 5 times, rib 3 sts.
This row creates eyelet holes to thread
ribbon through.

Work 3 rows in rib.
Cast off.

Dress back

Using blue yarn and 2.75mm (UK 12, US 2) needles,
cast on a picot edge as follows:

(Cast on 5 sts, cast off 2 sts) 13 times, cast on
2 sts [41 sts].

Knit 4 rows.

Next row: (K8, M1) 4 times, K9 [45 sts].

Change to 3.25mm (UK 10, US 3) needles and work
3 rows in SS.

Work fish design using orange yarn over next 3 rows.
Work all sts marked in **bold** using orange yarn and
the rest using blue yarn.

Row 1: (K5, **K1**, K1, **K3**) 4 times, K5.

Row 2: (P4, **P6**) 4 times, P5.

Row 3: as row 1.

Continue using blue yarn.

Starting with a WS row, work 13 rows in SS.

Next row: K2, (K2tog, K1) to last 4 sts, K2tog,
K2 [31 sts].

Starting with a WS row, work 5 rows in (K1, P1) rib.

Cast off 5 sts at beg of next 2 rows [21 sts].
Work 8 rows in (K1, P1) rib**.
Next row: work 7 sts in rib, cast off 7 sts, rib to end of row.
Turn, and working over first 7 sts, continue in rib until work measures 3cm (1¼in).
Next row: K1, P1, K2tog, yo, K1, P1, K1 [7 sts].
Work 1 row in rib.
Next row: K2tog, K1, P1, K1, K2tog [5 sts].
Cast off.
With RS facing, rejoin yarn to rem 7 sts and complete to match first side.

Dress front
Work as for back of dress to **.
Cast off.

Fish
Using orange yarn and 2.75mm (UK 12, US 2) needles, cast on 2 sts.
Next row: K1, M1, K1 [3 sts].
Purl 1 row.
Next row: (K1, M1) twice, K1 [5 sts].
Purl 1 row.
Next row: K2tog, K1, ssK [3 sts].
Purl 1 row.
Next row: sl1, K2tog, psso [1 st].
Next row: Kfbf [3 sts].
Next row: (K1, M1) twice, K1 [5 sts].
Knit 3 rows (the middle row forms a fold line)
Next row: P2tog, P1, P2tog [3 sts].
Next row: sl1, K2tog, psso [1 st].
Next row: Kfbf [3 sts].
Purl 1 row.
Next row: (K1, M1) twice, K1 [5 sts].
Purl 1 row.
Next row: K2tog, K1, ssK [3 sts].
Purl 1 row.
Next row: sl1, K2tog, psso [1 st].
Cast off rem st.

Shoes (make two)
Using blue yarn and 3.25mm (UK 10, US 3) needles, cast on 5 sts and knit 1 row.
Next row: K1, M1, knit to last st, M1, K1 [7 sts].
Knit 2 rows.
Rep the last 3 rows twice more [11 sts].
Work 2 rows in GS.
Cast on 13 sts at beg of next 2 rows [37 sts].

Shape shoe as follows:
Row 1: K13, K2tog, K7, ssK, K13 [35 sts].
Row 2: K12, K2tog, K7, ssK, K12 [33 sts].
Row 3: K11, K2tog, K7, ssK, K11 [31 sts].
Row 4: K10, K2tog, K7, ssK, K10 [29 sts].
Next row: K9, (K2tog) twice, K3, (ssK) twice, K9 [25 sts].
Cast off.

Strap for left shoe
Using blue yarn and 3.25mm (UK 10, US 3) needles, cast on 10 sts and knit 1 row.
Next row: K1, K2tog, yo, K7 [10 sts].
Knit 1 row.
Cast off.

Strap for right shoe
Using blue yarn and 3.25mm (UK 10, US 3) needles, cast on 10 sts and knit 1 row.
Next row: K7, yo, K2tog, K1 [10 sts].
Knit 1 row.
Cast off.

Making up
Join the front seam of the bloomers and then join the back seam, leaving a gap for the cat's tail. Thread ribbon through the eyelet holes in the ribbed top edge of the bloomers.

Join the side seams of the dress, sew the buttons to the top of the bib of the dress. Sew the fish together and stuff it gently with toy filling. Sew a ribbon bow to the bottom of the ribbed bib, attaching the fish to the bottom of the ribbon using the picture as guidance.

Sew the back seam of a shoe and sew the base in place. Attach the strap and sew a button to the shoe on the opposite side. Repeat for the second shoe.

Kitty Kat's night-time clothes

Materials

Pink 5-ply (sportweight) yarn
White 4-ply (fingering) Angora yarn
Three heart-shaped buttons
Black embroidery thread
Pink sewing cotton
Small amount of toy filling

Needles

3.25mm (UK 10, US 3) and 2.75mm
(UK 12, US 2) knitting needles
Sewing needle
Stitch holder

Tension

6 sts to 2.5cm (1in) measured over SS using
5-ply (sportweight) yarn and 3.25mm
(UK 10, US 3) needles

Pyjamas (left side)

Using pink yarn and 2.75mm (UK 12, US 2) needles,
cast on 26 sts and work 2 rows in (K1, P1) rib.
Change to white yarn and work 2 rows in SS.
Change to 3.25mm (UK 10, US 3) needles and pink
yarn. Work 8 rows in SS.
Next row: K1, M1, K11, M1, K2, M1, K11, M1,
K1 [30 sts].
Purl 1 row.
Next row: K1, M1, K13, M1, K2, M1, K13, M1,
K1 [34 sts].
Purl 1 row.
Next row: K1, M1, K15, M1, K2, M1, K15, M1,
K1 [38 sts].
Purl 1 row.
Next row: cast off 3 sts, K14, M1, K2, M1,
K18 [37 sts].
Next row: cast off 3 sts, purl to end of row [34 sts].
Next row: K1, K2tog, K13, M1, K2, M1, K13, ssK,
K1 [34 sts].
Next row: P1, P2togtbl, purl to last 3 sts, P2tog,
P1 [32 sts].
Next row: K15, M1, K2, M1, K15 [34 sts].
Work 15 rows in SS.

Next row: K14, K2tog, K2, ssK, K14 [32 sts].
Purl 1 row.
Next row: K13, K2tog, K2, ssK, K13 [30 sts].
Purl 1 row**.
Next row: K12, K2tog, K2, ssK, K12 [28 sts].
Next row: (WS) cast on 3 sts, (P1, K1) 3 times, purl to
end of row [31 sts].
Next row: K11, K2tog, K2, ssK, K8, (P1, K1)
3 times [29 sts].
Work sts as set for the next 3 rows (continuing the rib
pattern over the 6 edge sts).
Next row: K12, cast off 2 sts, K8, rib 6 sts as
set [27 sts].
Turn, working over the first 15 sts. From now on work
all rib sts as set.
Next row: rib 6 sts, P9.
Next row: K1, K2tog, K6, rib 6 sts [14 sts].
Next row: rib 6 sts, P8.
Next row: K1, K2tog, K5, rib 6 sts [13 sts].

Next row: rib 6 sts, P7.

Work 2 rows as set.

Next row: K7, place next 6 sts on a holder.

Work 2 rows in SS over these 7 sts only.

Next row: (WS) cast off 3 sts, purl to end of row [4 sts].

Knit 1 row.

Cast off rem 4 sts on WS.

With WS facing, rejoin yarn to 12 sts on holder and purl 1 row.

Next row: K9, ssK, K1 [11 sts].

Purl 1 row.

Next row: K8, ssK, K1 [10 sts].

Purl 1 row.

Work 6 rows in SS.

Next row: (RS) cast off 6 sts, knit to end of row [4 sts].

Purl 1 row.

Cast off rem 4 sts.

Pyjamas (right side)

Work as for left side to ** [30 sts].

Next row: cast on 3 sts, (K1, P1) 3 times, K9, K2tog, K2, ssK, K12 [31 sts].

Next row: purl to last 6 sts, rib 6 sts as set.

Next row: (K1, P1) 3 times, K8, K2tog, K2, ssK, K11 [29 sts].

Next row: purl to last 6 sts, rib 6 sts as set.

Next row: K1, P1, K2tog, yo, K1, P1, knit to end of row.

Next row: purl to last 6 sts, rib 6 sts as set.

From now on work all rib sts as set.

Next row: rib 6 sts, K9, cast off 2 sts, K11 [27 sts].

Turn, working over the first 12 sts and purl 1 row.

Next row: K1, K2tog, K9 [11 sts].

Purl 1 row.

Next row: K1, K2tog, K8 [10 sts].

Purl 1 row.

Work 7 rows in SS.

Next row: cast off 6 sts, purl to end of row [4 sts].

Knit 1 row.

Cast off rem 4 sts.

With WS facing, rejoin yarn to rem 15 sts, P9, rib 6 sts [15 sts].

Next row: rib 6 sts, K6, ssK, K1 [14 sts].

Next row: purl 8 sts, rib 6 sts.

Next row: K1, P1, K2tog, yo, K1, P1, K5, ssK, K1 [13 sts].

Work 3 rows as set.

Next row: rib 6 sts and place these sts on a holder, K7.

Next row: purl 7 sts on needle.

Next row: Cast off 3 sts, knit to end of row [4 sts].

Purl 1 row.

Cast off rem 4 sts.

Sleeves (make two)

Using pink yarn and 2.75mm (UK 12, US 2) needles, cast on 24 sts and work 2 rows in (K1, P1) rib.

Change to white yarn and work 2 rows in SS.

Change to 3.25mm (UK 10, US 3) needles and pink yarn.

Work 12 rows in SS.

Cast off.

Bunny's face (on front of pyjamas)

Using white yarn and 2.75mm (UK 12, US 2) needles, cast on 5 sts.

Next row: K1, M1, knit to last st, M1, K1 [7 sts].

Purl 1 row.

Rep last 2 rows twice more [11 sts].

Work 4 rows in SS.

Next row: K2tog, knit to last 2 sts, ssK [9 sts].

Purl 1 row.

Rep last 2 rows twice more [5 sts].

Cast off.

Bunny's ears (make two)

Using white yarn and 2.75mm (UK 12, US 2) needles, cast on 5 sts and work 8 rows in SS.

Next row: K2tog, K1, ssK [3 sts].

Purl 1 row.

Cast off.

Slippers (make two)

Worked in GS.

Using pink yarn and 3.25mm (UK 10, US 3) needles, cast on 5 sts and knit 1 row.

Next row: K1, M1, knit to last st, M1, K1 [7 sts].

Knit 2 rows.

Rep last 3 rows twice more [11 sts].

Knit 2 rows.

Cast on 13 sts at beg of next 2 rows [37 sts].

Shape slipper as follows:

Row 1: K13, K2tog, K7, ssK, K13 [35 sts].

Row 2: K12, K2tog, K7, ssK, K12 [33 sts].

Row 3: K11, K2tog, K7, ssK, K11 [31 sts].

Row 4: K10, K2tog, K7, ssK, K10 [29 sts].
Row 5: K9, (K2tog) twice, K3, (ssK) twice, K9 [25 sts].
Row 6: K8, (K2tog) twice, K1, (ssK) twice, K8 [21 sts].
Cast off.

Bunny ears on slippers (make four)
Using white yarn and 2.75mm (UK 12, US 2) needles, cast on 5 sts. Work 8 rows in SS.
Next row: K2tog, K1, ssK [3 sts].
Purl 1 row.
Next row: K1, M1, K1, M1, K1 [5 sts].
Purl 1 row.
Work 8 rows in SS.
Cast off.

Bunny tails on slippers (make two)
Using white yarn and 2.75mm (UK 12, US 2) needles, cast on 5 sts.
Next row: K1, M1, knit to last st, M1, K1 [7 sts].
Purl 1 row.
Rep last 2 rows twice more [11 sts].
Work 6 rows in SS.
Next row: K2tog, knit to last 3 sts, ssK [9 sts].
Purl 1 row.
Rep last 2 rows twice more [5 sts].
Thread yarn through rem 5 sts, gather edge of tail and pull into a 'ball', stuffing gently.

Making up
With RS together, join the pyjama shoulder seams. Join the back seam, leaving a hole for the cat's tail.

With RS of pyjamas facing and using 2.75mm (UK 12, US 2) needles and pink yarn, rib first 6 sts on holder as set, pick up and knit 6 sts up front collar edge, 12 sts across back of neck and 6 sts down front collar edge, rib 6 sts from holder [36 sts].

Change to white yarn and work 2 rows in rib as set in previous row.

Change to pink yarn and work in rib to last 4 sts, yo, P2tog, K1, P1. Work 1 row in (K1, P1) rib. Cast off loosely and evenly in rib.

Sew sleeve seams, side seams and leg seams.

Pin the bunny face to the front of the pyjamas, stuffing very slightly with toy filling to give it definition. Place the bunny ears behind the top edge of the face, using the picture as guidance. Sew the head and ears in place. Using black embroidery thread, embroider the bunny's eyes and nose. Using pink sewing cotton and

a sewing needle, sew the buttons in place to match buttonhole positions.

To make each slipper, sew the back seam together and sew the top of the slipper to the base. Fold an ear in half lengthways and sew the seams along the long sides. Repeat for a second ear. Sew two ears to the front of a slipper. Sew a bunny tail to the back seam of the slipper. Repeat for the second slipper.

Super Cat

Is it a bird? Is it a plane? No, it's Super Cat! Tough on the outside but soft in the middle, this has got to be the cuddliest super hero of all time.

Materials

Dark grey 5-ply (sportweight) yarn
Light grey 5-ply (sportweight) yarn
Red 8-ply (DK) yarn
Blue 8-ply (DK) yarn
Yellow 8-ply (DK) yarn
Small amount of black 4-ply (fingering) yarn
Two 10mm glass eyes
Toy filling
Chenille sticks for arms, legs and tail
Two small metal buttons with cat motif

Needles

3.25mm (UK 10, US 3) and 2.75mm
(UK 12, US 2) knitting needles
Two stitch markers

Tension

6 sts to 2.5cm (1in) measured over SS using
5-ply (sportweight) and 3.25mm (UK 10, US 3)
needles

Size

Approximately 18cm (7in) tall, from paws to top
of head

Body back

Using dark grey yarn and 3.25mm (UK 10, US 3)
needles, cast on 8 sts.
Row 1: K1, M1, knit to last st, M1, K1 [10 sts].
Row 2: P1, M1, purl to last st, M1, P1 [12 sts].
Rep last 2 rows once more [16 sts].
Rep row 1 once more [18 sts].
Work 11 rows in SS.
Next row: K1, K2tog, knit to last 3 sts, ssK,
K1 [16 sts].
Work 3 rows in SS.
Rep last 4 rows 4 more times [8 sts].
Cast off.

Help us, Super Cat, help us!

Don't despair! Super Cat will save you!

Body front

Using dark grey yarn and 3.25mm (UK 10, US 3) needles, cast on 8 sts and work 2 rows in SS.

Place markers 3 sts in from each end.

Row 1: K1, M1, knit to M, SM, M1, knit to M, M1, SM, knit to last st, M1, K1 [12 sts].

Row 2: P1, M1, purl to last st, M1, P1 [14 sts].

Rep last 2 rows twice more [26 sts].

Work 10 rows in SS.

Next row: K1, K2tog, knit to M, SM, K2tog, knit to 2 sts before M, ssK, SM, knit to last 3 sts, ssK, K1 [22 sts].

Remove markers.

Purl 1 row.

Rep last 2 rows once more [18 sts].

Next row: K1, K2tog, knit to last 3 sts, ssK, K1 [16 sts].

Work 3 rows in SS.

Rep last 4 rows 3 more times [10 sts].

Next row: K1, K2tog, knit to last 3 sts, ssK, K1 [8 sts].

P 1 row.

Cast off.

Head

Using dark grey yarn and 3.25mm (UK 10, US 3) needles, cast on 12 sts.

K1, M1, K5, M1, K5, M1, K1 [15 sts].

Purl 1 row.

Using the Fair Isle technique to carry the yarn, work as follows (see page 12). Work all sts in **bold** in light grey and all other sts in dark grey.

Next row: K6, M1, **K3**, M1, K6 [17 sts].

Next row: P1, M1, P6, **M1**, **P3**, **M1**, P6, M1, P1 [21 sts].

Next row: K8, **K1**, **M1**, **K3**, **M1**, **K1**, K8 [23 sts].

Next row: P1, M1, P7, **P2**, **M1**, **P3**, **M1**, **P2**, P7, M1, P1 [27 sts].

Next row: K9, **K3**, **M1**, **K3**, **M1**, **K3**, K9 [29 sts].

Next row: P9, **P11**, P9.

Next row: K9, **K11**, K9.

Next row: P9, **P11**, P9.

Next row: K9, **K2**, **K2tog**, **K3**, **ssK**, **K2**, K9 [27 sts].

Next row: P9, **P1**, **P2togtbl**, **P3**, **P2tog**, **P1**, P9 [25 sts].

Next row: K9, **K2togtbl**, **K3**, **K2tog**, K9 [23 sts].

Next row: P8, P2tog, **P3**, P2togtbl, P8 [21 sts].

Next row: K7, K2tog, **K3**, ssK, K7 [19 sts].

Next row: P6, P2togtbl, **P3**, P2tog, P6 [17 sts].

Next row: K1, K2tog, K5, **K1**, K5, ssK, K1 [15 sts].

This is the last row that uses light grey.

Next row: P1, P2togtbl, purl to last 3 sts, P2tog, P1 [13 sts].

Cast off 3 sts, K6, cast off rem 3 sts.

With WS facing, rejoin yarn to rem 7 sts and work 11 rows in SS.

Next row: K1, K2tog, K1, ssK, K1 [5 sts].

Work 3 rows in SS.

Next row: K2tog, K1, ssK [3 sts].

Purl 1 row.

Cast off.

Nose

Using black 4-ply (fingering) yarn and 2.75mm (UK 12, US 2) needles, cast on 5 sts and work 2 rows in SS.

Next row: K2tog, K1, ssK [3 sts].

Purl 1 row.

Next row: sl1, K2tog, psso.

Fasten off rem st.

Arms (make two)

Using dark grey yarn and 3.25mm (UK 10, US 3) needles, cast on 10 sts and work 12 rows in SS.

Change to light grey yarn and work 2 rows in SS.

Next row: K1, M1, K3, M1, K2, M1, K3, M1, K1 [14 sts].

Purl 1 row.

Next row: K1, M1, K5, M1, K2, M1, K5, M1, K1 [18 sts].

Purl 1 row.

Next row: K1, K2tog, K3, ssK, K2, K2tog, K3, ssK, K1 [14 sts].

Cast off on WS.

Feet (make two)

Using light grey yarn and 3.25mm (UK 10, US 3) needles, cast on 6 sts and knit 1 row.

Next row: P1, M1, purl to last st, M1, P1 [8 sts].

Next row: K1, M1, knit to last st, M1, K1 [10 sts].

Work 5 rows in SS.

Next row: K1, K2tog, knit to last 3 sts, ssK, K1 [8 sts].

Purl 1 row.

Next row: K1, M1, knit to last st, M1, K1 [10 sts].

Work 5 rows in SS.

Next row: K1, K2tog, knit to last 3 sts, ssK, K1 [8 sts].

Next row: P1, P2togtbl, purl to last 3 sts, P2tog, P1 [6 sts].

Knit 1 row.

Cast off on WS.

Legs (make two)

Using dark grey yarn and 3.25mm needles, cast on 10 sts and work 14 rows in SS.

Cast off.

Tail

Using dark grey yarn and 3.25mm (UK 10, US 3) needles, cast on 9 sts and work 7cm (2¾in) in SS.

Change to light grey yarn and work 2 rows in SS.

Next row: (K1, K2tog) 3 times [6 sts].

Purl 1 row.

Next row: (K2tog) 3 times [3 sts].

Thread yarn through rem sts and tighten.

Ears (make four)

Using dark grey yarn and 3.25mm (UK 10, US 3) needles, cast on 7 sts and work 2 rows in SS.

Next row: K2tog, knit to last 2 sts, ssK [5 sts].

Purl 1 row.

Rep last 2 rows once more [3 sts].

Next row: sl1, K2tog, psso [1 st].

Fasten off rem st.

Eye mask

Using blue yarn and 3.25mm (UK 10, US 3) needles, cast on 56 sts and knit 1 row.

Next row: P1, P2tog, purl to last 3 sts, P2tog, P1 [54 sts].

Next row: K1, K2tog, knit to last 3 sts, K2tog, K1 [52 sts].

Rep last 2 rows once more [48 sts].

Cast off loosely and evenly.

Making up

Sew the head seams together and stuff with toy filling. With WS together, sew two ear pieces together. Repeat for the second ear and sew both ears to the top of the head, using the picture as guidance.

Place the eye mask around the head and under the ears and pin to secure. Sew the eyes over the top of the eye mask and then sew the eye mask in place, folding the ends of the eye mask over each other to form a 'knot'.

Sew the nose in place and embroider the mouth and whiskers using black yarn. Using a needle and thread, sew from the base of the head to the back of each eye, pull the thread back down to the base and tighten. This gives a fantastic shape to the head.

Sew the side seams of the arms and the cast-off edges of the paws together. Place a chenille stick inside each of the arms. Stuff with toy filling and oversew two stitches on to the paws in light grey yarn to give the appearance of paws.

Sew each foot together, stuffing with toy filling as you go. Oversew two stitches as for the paws on the arms. Sew the side seam of each leg, insert a chenille stick and stuff with toy filling. Join each leg to a foot.

Pin the side seams of the body together. Pin the arms into the side seams approximately 1.5cm (½in) from the top and pin the legs into the bottom seam, making sure you leave a 4–5 stitch gap between the legs to allow for fitting the outfit.

Sew the side seams of the body, sewing the arms and legs into the seams. Stuff with toy filling as you go. Sew the head to the top of the body.

Sew the side seam of the tail, add a chenille stick and stuff with toy filling. Sew to the back of the cat using the picture as guidance, approximately 2cm (¾in) up from the bottom seam.

Super Cat's outfit

Front

Using red yarn and 3.25mm (UK 10, US 3) needles, cast on 4 sts and work 2 rows in SS.

Next row: K1, M1, knit to last st, M1, K1 [6 sts].

Purl 1 row.

Rep last 2 rows once more [8 sts].

Row 1: K1, M1, knit to last st, M1, K1 [10 sts].

Row 2: P1, M1, purl to last st, M1, P1 [12 sts].

Rep last 2 rows 3 more times [24 sts].

Rep row 1 once more [26 sts].

Work 5 rows in SS.

Next row: K1, K2tog, knit to last 3 sts, ssK, K1 [24 sts].

Purl 1 row.

Rep last 2 rows once more [22 sts].

Change to blue yarn.

Next row: K1, K2tog, knit to last 3 sts, ssK, K1 [20 sts].

Purl 1 row.

Rep last 2 rows once more [18 sts].

Work 4 rows in SS.

**Next row: cast off 2 sts, K4, cast off 4 sts, K4, cast off 2 sts, leaving you with 2 groups of 5 sts.

***With WS facing, rejoin yarn to one side and purl 1 row.

Next row: K2tog, P1, ssK [3 sts].

Work 4 rows in SS.

Cast off on WS*.

Rejoin yarn to other side and work from * to * to match first side.

Back

Using red yarn and 3.25mm (UK 10, US 3) needles, cast on 4 sts and work 2 rows in SS.

Next row: K1, M1, knit to last st, M1, K1 [6 sts].

Purl 1 row.

Rep last 2 rows once more [8 sts].

Row 1: K1, M1, knit to last st, M1, K1 [10 sts].

Row 2: P1, M1, purl to last st, M1, P1 [12 sts].

Row 3: K1, M1, K4, cast off 2 sts, K3, M1, K1 [12 sts].

Row 4: P1, M1, P5, cast on 2 sts, P5, M1, P1 [16 sts].

Row 5: K1, M1, knit to last st, M1, K1 [18 sts].

Row 6: P1, M1, purl to last st, M1, P1 [20 sts].

Rep rows 5 and 6 once more [24 sts].

Rep row 5 once more [26 sts].

Work 5 rows in SS.

Next row: K1, K2tog, knit to last 3 sts, ssK, K1 [24 sts].

Purl 1 row.

Rep last 2 rows once more [22 sts].

Change to blue yarn.

Next row: K1, K2tog, knit to last 3 sts, ssK, K1 [20 sts].

Purl 1 row.

Rep last 2 rows once more [18 sts].

Work 4 rows in SS.

Complete back by working as for front from ** to end.

Cape

Using red yarn and 3.25mm (UK 10, US 3) needles, cast on 40 sts and work 2 rows in SS.

Next row: K1, K2tog, knit to last 3 sts, ssK, K1 [38 sts].

Purl 1 row.

Rep last 2 rows a further 13 times until 14 sts rem.

Next row: K4, cast off 6 sts, K3 [8 sts].

Turn and, working on first set of 4 sts, work 9 rows in SS.

Next row: K2tog, turn and cast on 2 sts, turn, K2tog [4 sts].

Purl 1 row.

Next row: K1, K2tog, K1 [3 sts].

Cast off.

With RS facing, rejoin yarn to second set of 4 sts and work 10 rows in SS.

Next row: K1, K2tog, K1 [3 sts].

Cast off.

Using red yarn and 3.25mm (UK 10, US 3) needles, with RS facing, pick up and knit 30 sts along bottom edge of cape. Cast off knitwise. With RS facing, pick up and knit 31 sts along side edge of cape and 3 sts across top of tie. Cast off knitwise. With RS facing, pick up and knit 3 sts across top of other tie and 31 sts down front edge. Cast off. With RS facing, pick up and knit 28 sts around inside neck edge of cape. Cast off knitwise.

Belt

Using yellow yarn and 3.25mm (UK 10, US 3) needles, cast on 4 sts and work in SS until belt fits around middle of outfit, covering colour change.

Making up

Press all outfit pieces lightly. This will make them easier to sew together. Sew the bottom seam of the outfit and, with RS facing and using yellow yarn and 3.25mm (UK 10, US 3) needles, pick up and knit 12 sts along the front leg edge and 12 sts along the back leg edge. Cast off knitwise. Repeat for the second leg.

Using yellow yarn and starting at the middle front of the outfit where the red and blue join, embroider an upside-down 'Y' on the front of the pants using chain stitch (see page 13) and using the picture as guidance.

Join the side seams of the outfit. Using yellow yarn and 3.25mm (UK 10, US 3) needles, with RS facing pick up and knit 7 sts up the front armhole edge

and 7 sts down the back armhole edge. Cast off knitwise. Repeat for the second armhole.

Using yellow yarn and 3.25mm (UK 10, US 3) needles, with RS facing pick up and knit 18 sts around the front neck edge. Cast off knitwise. Pick up and knit 15 sts around the back neck edge. Cast off knitwise. Sew all the ends in securely. Join one shoulder seam.

Put the outfit over the cat's head and pull it down towards the legs. Insert the tail into the hole made at the back of the outfit. Sew the remaining shoulder seam.

Fit the belt and sew it in place. Stitch a button on the front of the belt. Sew a second button on to the cape tie, place the cape on the cat and button it up.

Clematis

If you love flowers, you will love this floral feline. Knit her and stitch her, then display her proudly in your home – a beautiful little cat you simply won't want to part with!

Materials

Dark grey 12-ply (chunky) yarn,
2 x 50g (2oz) balls
Pink 2-ply (laceweight) yarn
Self-patterning 4-ply (fingering) yarn
Two 10mm glass eyes
Toy filling
Chenille sticks
Strong black sewing thread

Needles

5.5mm (UK 5, US 9) and 2.75mm (UK 12, US 2)
knitting needles
Stitch holder

Tension

4 sts to 2.5cm (1in) measured over SS and using
5.5mm (UK 5, US 9) needles

Size

Approximately 36cm (14¼in) long, from tip
of tail to front paws

Body

Worked in one piece from tip of tail.

Using dark grey yarn and 5.5mm (UK 5, US 9) needles, cast on 4 sts and work 2 rows in SS.

Next row: K1, M1, knit to last st, M1, K1 [6 sts].

Purl 1 row.

Rep last 2 rows twice more [10 sts].

Work 6 rows in SS.

Shape tail as follows:

Row 1: K8, w&t.

Row 2: P6, w&t.

Row 3: knit to end of row.

Work 3 rows in SS.

Rep last 7 rows 4 more times.

Work 4 rows in SS.

Next row: cast off 4 sts, K3, cast off 3 sts [4 sts].

Cast on 8 sts at beg of next 2 rows [20 sts].

Purl 1 row.

Next row: K1, M1, knit to last st, M1, K1 [22 sts].

Next row: P1, M1, purl to last st, M1, P1 [24 sts].

Next row: K19, w&t.

P14, w&t.

Next row: knit to end of row.

Purl 1 row.

Next row: K1, M1, knit to last st, M1, K1 [26 sts].

Next row: P1, M1, purl to last st, M1, P1 [28 sts].

**Next row: K23, w&t.

P18, w&t.

Next row: knit to end of row.

Purl 1 row**.

Rep from ** to ** twice more.

Next row: K1, M1, knit to last st, M1, K1 [30 sts].

Work 11 rows in SS.

Stitches are now divided for front legs and body.

Next row: K5, cast off 5, K9, cast off 5, K4.

Turn and working over first 5 sts only, P5. Leave rem sts on a holder.

Cast on 6 sts at beg of next row, knit to end of row [11 sts].

***Starting with a purl row, work 9 rows in SS.

Next row: K3, (K2tog) twice, K4 [9 sts].

Next row: P2, (P2tog) twice, P3 [7 sts].

Thread yarn through rem sts and fasten off***.

With RS facing, rejoin yarn to 5 sts at other end of knitting on holder (second leg) and knit 1 row.

Cast on 6 sts at beg of next row [11 sts].

Knit 1 row.

Work from *** to *** as for first leg.

With RS facing, rejoin yarn to centre 10 sts on holder and work as follows:

K2, K2tog, K2, ssK, K2 [8 sts].

Work 5 rows in SS.

Next row: K1, M1, knit to last st, M1, K1 [10 sts].

Purl 1 row.

Rep last 2 rows twice more [14 sts].

Work 10 rows in SS.

Next row: K1, M1, knit to last st, M1, K1 [16 sts].

Purl 1 row.

Rep last 2 rows once more [18 sts].

Work 10 rows in SS.

Next row: K1, K2tog, knit to last 3 sts, ssK, K1 [16 sts].

Purl 1 row.

Rep last 2 rows once more [14 sts].

Work 4 rows in SS.

Next row: K1, K2tog, knit to last 3 sts, ssK, K1 [12 sts].

Work 5 rows in SS.

Next row: K1, K2tog, knit to last 3 sts, ssK, K1 [10 sts].

Purl 1 row.

Rep last 2 rows once more [8 sts].

Next row: K1, K2tog, K2, ssK, K1 [6 sts].

Next row: P1, P2togtbl, P2tog, P1 [4 sts].

Cast off.

Head

Using dark grey yarn and 5.5mm (UK 5, US 9) needles, cast on 20 sts and purl 1 row.

Next row: K4, M1, K1, M1, K4, M1, K2, M1, K4, M1, K1, M1, K4 [26 sts].

Purl 1 row.

Next row: K5, M1, K1, K2tog, K4, M1, K2, M1, K4, ssK, K1, M1, K5 [28 sts].

Purl 1 row.

Next row: K6, M1, K1, K2tog, K4, M1, K2, M1, K4, ssK, K1, M1, K6 [30 sts].

Purl 1 row.

Next row: K14, M1, K2, M1, K14 [32 sts].

Purl 1 row.

Next row: K15, M1, K2, M1, K15 [34 sts].

Purl 1 row.

Next row: K16, M1, K2, M1, K16 [36 sts].

Purl 1 row.

Next row: K15, K2tog, K2, ssK, K15 [34 sts].

Next row: P14, P2togtbl, P2, P2tog, P14 [32 sts].
Next row: K13, K2tog, K2, ssK, K13 [30 sts].
Purl 1 row.
Next row: K11, K2tog, K4, ssK, K11 [28 sts].
Purl 1 row.
Next row: K1, K2tog, knit to last 3 sts, ssK, K1 [26 sts].
Next row: P1, P2togtbl, purl to last 3 sts, P2tog, P1 [24 sts].
Next row: K4, K2tog, ssK, K8, ssK, K2tog, K4 [20 sts].
Next row: P3, P2tog, P2togtbl, P6, P2togtbl, P2tog, P3 [16 sts].
Next row: K2, K2tog, ssK, K4, ssK, K2tog, K2 [12 sts].
Cast off rem sts on WS.

Ears (make two)

Using dark grey yarn and 5.5mm (UK 5, US 9) needles, cast on 8 sts.

Work 2 rows in SS.

Next row: K1, K2tog, K2, ssK, K1 [6 sts].

Purl 1 row.

Next row: K1, K2tog, ssK, K1 [4 sts].

Purl 1 row.

Next row: K2tog, ssK [2 sts].

Next row: P2tog.

Fasten off rem st.

Ear linings (make two)

Using a double strand of pink yarn and 2.75mm (UK 12, US 2) needles, cast on 10 sts.

Work 2 rows in SS.

Next row: K1, K2tog, knit to last st, ssK, K1 [8 sts].

Purl 1 row.

Rep the last 2 rows twice more [4 sts].

Next row: K2tog, ssK [2 sts].

Next row: P2tog.

Fasten off rem st.

Nose

Using a double strand of pink yarn and 2.75mm (UK 12, US 2) needles, cast on 5 sts.

Work 2 rows in SS.

Next row: K2tog, K1, K2tog [3 sts].

Next row: sl1, P2tog, psso [1 st].

Fasten off rem st.

Back leg (right)

**Using grey yarn and 5.5mm (UK 5, US 9) needles, cast on 7 sts and knit 1 row.

Next row: P1, M1, purl to last st, M1, P1 [9 sts].

Next row: K1, M1, knit to last st, M1, K1 [11 sts].

Starting with a purl row, work 7 rows in SS**.

Next row: cast off 5 sts, K1, M1, knit to last st, M1, K1 [8 sts].

Next row: P1, M1, purl to last st, M1, P1 [10 sts].

Next row: K1, M1, knit to last st, M1, K1 [12 sts].

Rep last 2 rows once more [16 sts].

Work 7 rows in SS.

Row 1: K1, ssK, knit to last 3 sts, K2tog, K1 [14 sts].

Row 2: purl.

Rep rows 1 and 2 once more and row 1 once more [10 sts].

Next row: (P1, P2tog) 3 times, P1 [7 sts].

Cast off rem sts.

Back leg (left)

Follow instructions for right back leg from ** to **.

Knit 1 row.

Next row: cast off 5 sts, P1, M1, purl to last st, M1, P1 [8 sts].

Next row: K1, M1, knit to last st, M1, K1 [10 sts].

Next row: P1, M1, purl to last st, M1, P1 [12 sts].

Rep last 2 rows once more [16 sts].

Work 7 rows in SS.

Row 1: (WS) P1, P2togtbl, purl to last 3 sts, P2tog, P1 [14 sts].

Row 2: knit.

Rep rows 1 and 2 once more and then row 1 once more [10 sts].

Next row: (K1, K2tog) 3 times, K1 [7 sts].

Cast off rem sts.

Making up

Sew the side seams of the front legs. Stuff the front legs with toy filling. Fold the narrow middle front section of the cat downwards. Sew the edge of the middle section to the cast-off edge down towards the front legs. Continue sewing under the legs to the side of the body then towards the tail, stuffing with toy filling as you go. Sew the cast-on stitches of the front legs to the front of the body, using the picture as guidance.

Sew the tail seam, sliding a piece of chenille stick in as you go. Sew the base of the tail to the body.

Attach the safety eyes to the head and sew the back seam of the head. Stuff with toy filling. With WS together, sew an ear lining to each ear using pink yarn. Sew the ears to the top of the head. Using pink yarn, sew the nose in place, stitch on the mouth and sew the head to the body.

Sew the lower part of each back leg together and stuff gently. Pin the back legs in place, with the lower leg pointing downwards. Fold the lower leg up to lay along the side seam of the body. Use the picture as guidance. Sew in place, stitching the inside of the lower leg to the side of the body.

Flowers

Petals (make eleven)

Using 2.75mm (UK 12, US 2) needles and self-patterning yarn, cast on 4 sts and purl 1 row.

Next row: K1, M1, knit to last st, M1, K1 [6 sts].

Purl 1 row.

Rep last 2 rows once more [8 sts].

Work 2 rows in SS.

Next row: K2tog, knit to last 2 sts, ssK [6 sts].

Next row: P2tog, P2, P2togtbl [4 sts].

Cast off.

Flower centres (make three)

Using 2.75mm (UK 12, US 2) needles and self-patterning yarn, cast on 1 st.

Row 1: Kfbf [3 sts].

Row 2: (Kfb) 3 times [6 sts].

Starting with a knit row, work 4 rows in SS.

Row 7: (K2tog) 3 times [3 sts].

Row 8: sl1, K2tog, psso [1 st].

Fasten off rem st.

Leaves (make nine)

Using 2.75mm (UK 12, US 2) needles and self-patterning yarn, cast on 3 sts and purl 1 row.

Next row: (K1, yo) twice, K1 [5 sts].

Purl 1 row.

Next row: K2, yo, K1, yo, K2 [7 sts].

Purl 1 row.

Next row: K3, yo, K1, yo, K3 [9 sts].

Purl 1 row.

Next row: K3, sl1, K2tog, psso, K3 [7 sts].

Purl 1 row.

Next row: K2, sl1, K2tog, psso, K2 [5 sts].

Purl 1 row.

Next row: K1, sl1, K2tog, psso, K1 [3 sts].

Next row: sl1, K2tog, psso [1 st].

Fasten off rem st.

Making up

Pin the petals, flower centres and leaves into place using the picture on page 65 as guidance and sew them in place using the self-patterning yarn. Using green self-patterning yarn, embroider using chain stitch and French knots (see pages 12 and 13).

Valentino

Romance is in the air for Valentino. He's got a big heart (and a belly to match), and his irresistible charm means you will fall head over heels in love with him. A perfect gift for your Valentine! Instructions for the mice are provided on page 110.

Materials
Black sparkly 2-ply (laceweight) yarn
(use double throughout)
Red 4-ply (fingering) yarn
Pale pink 2-ply (laceweight) yarn
Green 4-ply (fingering) yarn
Toy filling
Two 6mm glass eyes
Chenille stick

Needles
2.75mm (UK 12, US 2) and 2mm (UK 14, US 0)
knitting needles

Tension
8 sts to 2.5cm (1in) measured over SS
using 2.75mm (UK 12, US 2) needles

Size
Approximately 13cm (5in) tall

Body (make two)
Using a double strand of black yarn and 2.75mm (UK 12, US 2) needles, cast on 28 sts and work 2 rows in SS.
Next row: K1, M1, knit to last st, M1, K1 [30 sts].
Purl 1 row.
Rep the last 2 rows 3 more times [36 sts].
Work 16 rows in SS.
Next row: K1, K2tog, knit to last 3 sts, ssK, K1 [34 sts].
Purl 1 row.
Rep the last 2 rows 4 more times [26 sts].
Next row: K1, K2tog, knit to last 3 sts, ssK, K1 [24 sts].
Next row: P1, P2togtbl, purl to last 3 sts, P2tog, P1 [22 sts].

I love you!

I love you too!

Rep the last 2 rows twice more [14 sts].

Work 8 rows in SS.

Next row: K1, K2tog, knit to last 3 sts, ssK, K1 [12 sts].

Purl 1 row.

Rep the last 2 rows once more [10 sts].

Next row: K1, K2tog, knit to last 3 sts, ssK, K1 [8 sts].

Next row: P1, P2togtbl, purl to last 3 sts, P2tog, P1 [6 sts].

Cast off.

Base

Using a double strand of black yarn and 2.75mm (UK 12, US 2) needles, cast on 20 sts and work 2 rows in SS.

Row 1: K1, M1, knit to last st, M1, K1 [22 sts].

Row 2: P1, M1, purl to last st, M1, P1 [24 sts].

Rep last 2 rows twice more [28 sts].

Work 4 rows in SS.

Next row: K1, K2tog, knit to last 3 sts, ssK, K1 [26 sts].

Next row: P1, P2togtbl, purl to last 3 sts, P2tog, P1 [24 sts].

Rep last 2 rows twice more [20 sts].

Work 2 rows in SS.

Cast off.

Arms (make two)

Using a double strand of black yarn and 2.75mm (UK 12, US 2) needles, cast on 10 sts and work 8 rows in SS.

Next row: K1, K2tog, knit to last 3 sts, ssK, K1 [8 sts].

Purl 1 row.

Cast off.

Fingers and toes (make four)

Using a double strand of black yarn and 2.75mm (UK 12, US 2) needles, cast on 2 sts.

Row 1: (Kfb) twice [4 sts].

Row 2: (Kfb) 4 times [8 sts].

Row 3: knit.

Row 4: (P2tog) 4 times [4 sts].

Row 5: (K2tog) twice [2 sts].

Row 6: purl.

Rep these 6 rows twice more to make 3 toes.

Cast off rem 2 sts.

Heart

Using red yarn and 2.75mm (UK 12, US 2) needles, cast on 2 sts.

Next row: (Kfb) twice [4 sts].

Purl 1 row.

Next row: K1, M1, knit to last st, M1, K1 [6 sts].

Purl 1 row.

Rep last 2 rows 7 more times [20 sts].

Next row: K1, K2tog, K4, ssK, K1 [8 sts].

Turn, working only one side of the heart.

*Purl 1 row.

Next row: K1, K2tog, K2, ssK, K1 [6 sts].

Purl 1 row.

Next row: K1, K2tog, ssK, K1 [4 sts].

Next row: P2togtbl, P2tog [2 sts].

Cast off*.

With RS facing, rejoin yarn to rem 10 sts.

Next row: K1, K2tog, K4, ssK, K1 [8 sts].

Work as for other side of heart from * to *.

Tail

Using a double strand of black yarn and 2.75mm (UK 12, US 2) needles, cast on 8 sts and work 8 rows in SS.

*Next row: K6, w&t.

Next row: P4, w&t.

Next row: knit to end of row.

Purl 1 row*.

Rep from * to * a further 3 times.

Work 12 rows in SS.

Next row: K1, K2tog, knit to last 3 sts, ssK, K1 [6 sts].

Purl 1 row.

Next row: K1, K2tog, ssK, K1 [4 sts].

Thread yarn though rem sts and fasten off.

Ears (make two)

Using a double strand of black yarn and 2.75mm (UK 12, US 2) needles, cast on 5 sts and work 2 rows in SS.

Next row: K1, sl1, K2tog, psso, K1 [3 sts].

Purl 1 row.

Next row: sl1, K2tog, psso.

Thread yarn through rem st.

Ear linings (make two)

Using pink yarn and 2mm (UK 14, US 0) needles, cast on 5 sts and work 2 rows in SS.

Next row: K1, sl1, K2tog, psso, K1 [3 sts].

Purl 1 row.

Next row: sl1, K2tog, psso.

Thread yarn through rem st.

Rosebud

Using green yarn and 2.75mm (UK 12, US 2) needles, cast on 16 sts and knit 1 row.

Change to red yarn and work 3 rows in SS.

Next row: K13, w&t.

Purl 1 row.

Next row: K10, w&t.

Purl 1 row.

Next row: K6, w&t.

Purl 1 row.

Cast off, picking up 'wraps' and knitting them together with sts on needle. Roll rose petal sideways from smallest side to largest side to form bud and stitch to hold in place.

Rosebud stem

Using green yarn and 2.75mm (UK 12, US 2) needles, cast on 3 sts.

Work in SS until stem measures 5cm (2in) long.

Thread yarn through sts and fasten off.

Sew side seam and sew to base of rosebud.

Alternatively, work the stem as an i-cord (see page 12).

Leaves (make two)

Using green yarn and 2.75mm (UK 12, US 2) needles, cast on 2 sts.

Next row: K1, M1, K1 [3 sts].

Knit 1 row.

Next row: K1, M1, K1, M1, K1 [5 sts].

Knit 3 rows.

Next row: K2tog, K1, ssK [3 sts].

Knit 1 row.

Next row: sl1, K2tog, psso [1 st].

Fasten off rem st and sew leaves to stem of rosebud.

Making up

Using the picture as a guide, position the cat's eyes and sew them in place. Join the side seams of the body, stuffing with toy filling as you go. Sew the base in place. Sew the side seams of the arms.

Run a thread around each of the three fingers/toes of the paws and gather. Repeat for all four paws. Stitch a paw to the end of each arm, and two paws to the base of the cat where the front cast-on seam and the base join. Stuff the arms gently and sew them to the sides of the body.

Sew the ear linings to the ears and attach the ears to the top of the head.

Sew the side seam of the tail, place a chenille stick inside and sew it to the side of the body. Using green yarn, sew the rosebud to the paw on the opposite side to the tail.

Embroider a French knot (see page 12) for the nose using a double strand of pink 2-ply (laceweight) yarn. Embroider the mouth.

Sew the heart to the belly, stuffing it slightly with toy filling to give definition.

Monster Cat

A freak of nature he might be, but for those of us with a quirky sense of humour he's the perfect pet. Let your imagination run wild and design your own cat-like creature that's not quite as cute as the real thing, but definitely just as cuddly.

Materials

1 ball each of 5-ply (sportweight) yarn in blue, brown, yellow and orange
Toy filling
One 2.5cm (1in) button with four holes
Brown felt

Needles

3.25mm (UK 10, US 3) knitting needles

Tension

6 sts to 2.5cm (1in) measured over SS

Size

Approximately 16cm (6¼in) tall to top of head

Front

Worked in SS.

Using blue yarn, cast on 40 sts and work 16 rows.
Carrying blue yarn up the side of the work, change to brown yarn and work 6 rows.
Change to yellow and work 6 rows.
Change to brown and work a further 6 rows.
Change to blue and work 22 rows**.
Next row: K14, cast off 15, K10 [25 sts].
Turn and, working over first 11 sts, purl 1 row.
Row 1: K1, K2tog, knit to end of row [10 sts].
Row 2: purl.
Repeat the last 2 rows 3 more times [4 sts].
Rep row 1 and cast off rem 3 sts on the WS.
With WS facing, rejoin yarn to rem 14 sts and purl 1 row. Work 2 rows in SS.
Next row: K1, K2tog, knit to last 3 sts, ssK, K1 [12 sts].
Purl 1 row.
Rep last 2 rows 4 more times [4 sts].
Next row: K1, K2tog, K1 [3 sts].
Cast off.

Back

Work as for front to **.
Next row: K11, cast off 15, K13 [25 sts].
Turn and, working over first 14 sts, purl 1 row.
Work 2 rows in SS.
Next row: K1, K2tog, knit to last 3 sts, ssK, K1 [12 sts].
Purl 1 row.
Rep last 2 rows 4 more times [4 sts].
Next row: K1, K2tog, K1 [3 sts].
Cast off.

With WS facing, rejoin yarn to rem 11 sts, purl 1 row.

Row 1: knit to last 3 sts, ssK, K1 [10 sts].

Row 2: purl.

Repeat the last 2 rows 3 more times [4 sts].

Rep row 1 and cast off rem 3 sts on the WS.

Base

Using blue yarn, cast on 30 sts and work 2 rows in SS.

Row 1: K1, M1, knit to last st, M1, K1 [32 sts].

Row 2: purl.

Rep last 2 rows 3 more times [38 sts].

Work 4 rows in SS.

Next row: K1, K2tog, knit to last 3 sts, ssK, K1 [36 sts].

Purl 1 row.

Rep last 2 rows 3 more times [30 sts].

Cast off.

Arms (make two)

Using blue yarn, cast on 12 sts and work 10 rows in SS.

Next row: K1, K2tog, knit to last 3 sts, ssK, K1 [10 sts].

Purl 1 row.

Work the last 2 rows once more [8 sts].

Next row: K1, M1, knit to last st, M1, K1 [10 sts].

Purl 1 row.

Rep last 2 rows once more [12 sts].

Work 10 rows in SS.

Cast off.

Feet (make two)

Using brown yarn, cast on 12 sts and work 8 rows in SS.

Next row: K1, K2tog, knit to last 3 sts, ssK, K1 [10 sts].

Purl 1 row.

Work the last 2 rows once more [8 sts].

Next row: K1, M1, knit to last st, M1, K1 [10 sts].

Purl 1 row.

Rep last 2 rows once more [12 sts].

Work 8 rows in SS.

Cast off.

Belly

Using orange yarn, cast on 10 sts and work 2 rows in SS.

Row 1: K1, M1, knit to last st, M1, K1 [12 sts].

Row 2: P1, M1, purl to last st, M1, P1 [14 sts].

Rep last 2 rows once more [18 sts].

Next row: K1, M1, knit to last st, M1, K1 [20 sts].

Purl 1 row.

Rep last 2 rows once more [22 sts].

Work 10 rows in SS.

Next row: K1, K2tog, knit to last 3 sts, ssK, K1 [20 sts].

Purl 1 row.

Rep last 2 rows once more [18 sts].

Next row: K1, K2tog, knit to last 3 sts, ssK, K1 [16 sts].

Next row: P1, P2togtbl, purl to last 3 sts, P2tog, P1 [14 sts].

Rep last 2 rows once more [10 sts].

Cast off.

Tail

Using blue yarn, cast on 22 sts and work 10 rows in SS.

Change to brown and work 4 rows.

Work 4 rows in yellow and a further 4 rows in brown.

Change to blue and continue in SS until work measures 12cm (4¼in) from end of last brown stripe.

Next row: K1, K2tog, K5, ssK, K2, K2tog, K5, ssK, K1.

Purl 1 row.

Next row: K1, K2tog, K3, ssK, K2, K2tog, K3, ssK, K1.

Purl 1 row.

Cast off.

Making up

Fold the arms in half and sew the side seams, with one arm having the WS on the outside and the other with the RS on the outside to provide contrast. Repeat with the feet.

Sew the tail seam and gently stuff the end of the tail. Tie a knot in the tail as shown in the picture. Gently stuff the rest of the tail.

Pin the arms and tail in position on the body using the picture as a guide and join the side seams, sewing the arms and tail into the side seams as you join. Stuff with toy filling. Pin the feet in position on the front of the body and sew them into the front seam where the front and base join, gently topping up with stuffing if required as you close.

Cut out the felt eye using the button as a template to make each eye the same size. Sew on the button and the felt circle using different-coloured yarn for each one and sewing an 'X' in the centre of the felt eye.

Sew the belly to the front of the cat using orange yarn and big stitches to add detail. Using yellow yarn, embroider three 'claws' to each arm. Using orange yarn, embroider three 'claws' to each foot.

Am I scary from the back too?

Fluffy Cat

Small, sweet and very, very fluffy, this cute kitten is quick to knit and won't ever grow up! Instructions for the mice are provided on page 110.

Materials

White 4-ply (fingering) Angora yarn
Pale pink 2-ply (laceweight) yarn
Two 8mm plastic safety eyes, painted on the backs with silver nail polish
Toy filling
Pink ribbon
Chenille stick
Strong sewing thread

Needles

2.75mm (UK 12, US 2) and 2mm (UK 14, US 0) knitting needles
Stitch holder

Tension

7–8 sts to 2.5cm (1in) measured over SS using 2.75mm (UK 12, US 2) needles

Size

Approximately 18cm (7in) long, from tip of tail to front paws

Body

Worked in one piece from tip of tail.

NB: after working the short row shaping on the back of the body and reaching a wrapped stitch, pick up the wrap and knit or purl with the stitch it is wrapped around. This gives a very neat result.

Using white yarn and 2.75mm (UK 12, US 2) needles, cast on 4 sts and work 2 rows in SS.

Next row: K1, M1, K2, M1, K1 [6 sts].

Work 2 rows in SS.

*Next row: P5, w&t.

Next row: K4, w&t.

Next row: purl to end of row.

Knit 1 row*.

Work from * to * a further 10 times.

Cast off 1 st at beg of next 2 rows.

Next row: cast on 8 sts, purl across 12 sts on needle, turn and cast on 8 sts [20 sts].

Work 2 rows in SS.

Next row: K1, M1, knit to last st, M1, K1 [22 sts].

Next row: P1, M1, purl to last st, M1, P1 [24 sts].

Next row: K19, w&t.

P14, w&t.

Next row: knit to end of row.

Purl 1 row.

Next row: K1, M1, knit to last st, M1, K1 [26 sts].

Next row: P1, M1, purl to last st, M1, P1 [28 sts].

**Next row: K23, w&t.

P18, w&t.

Next row: knit to end of row.

Purl 1 row**.

Rep from ** to ** twice more.

Next row: K1, M1, knit to last st, M1, K1 [30 sts].

Work 11 rows in SS.

The stitches are now divided for the two front legs and the body.

Next row: K4, cast off 6, K9, cast off 6, K3.

Turn and, working over first 4 sts only, P4. Leave rem sts on a holder.

Cast on 6 sts at beg of next row and knit to end of row [10 sts].

***Starting with a purl row, work 9 rows in SS.

Next row: K3, (K2tog) twice, K3 [8 sts].

Next row: P2, (P2tog) twice, P2 [6 sts].

Thread yarn through rem sts and fasten off***.

With RS facing, rejoin yarn to 4 sts at other end of knitting on holder (second leg) and knit 1 row.

Cast on 6 sts at beg of next row and purl to end of row [10 sts].

Knit 1 row.

Work from *** to *** as for first leg.

With RS facing, rejoin yarn to centre 10 sts on holder and work as follows:

K2, K2tog, K2, ssK, K2 [8 sts].

Work 5 rows in SS.

Next row: K1, M1, knit to last st, M1, K1 [10 sts].

Purl 1 row.

Rep last 2 rows once more [12 sts].

Work 12 rows in SS.

Next row: K1, M1, knit to last st, M1, K1 [14 sts].

Purl 1 row.

Rep last 2 rows once more [16 sts].

Work 4 rows in SS.

Next row: K1, K2tog, knit to last 3 sts, ssK, K1 [14 sts].

Purl 1 row.

Rep last 2 rows once more [12 sts].

Work 4 rows in SS.

Next row: K1, K2tog, knit to last 3 sts, ssK, K1 [10 sts].

Work 5 rows in SS.

Next row: K1, K2tog, knit to last 3 sts, ssK, K1 [8 sts].

Purl 1 row.

Next row: K1, K2tog, knit to last 3 sts, ssK, K1 [6 sts].

Next row: P1, P2togtbl, P2tog, P1 [4 sts].

Cast off.

Head

Using white yarn and 2.75mm (UK 12, US 2) needles, cast on 20 sts and purl 1 row.

Next row: K4, M1, K1, M1, K4, M1, K2, M1, K4, M1, K1, M1, K4 [26 sts].

Purl 1 row.

Next row: K5, M1, K1, K2tog, K4, M1, K2, M1, K4, ssK, K1, M1, K5 [28 sts].

Purl 1 row.

Next row: K6, M1, K1, K2tog, K4, M1, K2, M1, K4, ssK, K1, M1, K6 [30 sts].

Purl 1 row.

Next row: K14, M1, K2, M1, K14 [32 sts].

Purl 1 row.

Next row: K15, M1, K2, M1, K15 [34 sts].

Purl 1 row.

Next row: K16, M1, K2, M1, K16 [36 sts].

Purl 1 row.

Next row: K15, K2tog, K2, ssK, K15 [34 sts].

Next row: P14, P2togtbl, P2, P2tog, P14 [32 sts].

Next row: K13, K2tog, K2, ssK, K13 [30 sts].

Purl 1 row.

Next row: K11, K2tog, K4, ssK, K11 [28 sts].

Purl 1 row.

Next row: K1, K2tog, knit to last 3 sts, ssK, K1 [26 sts].

Next row: P1, P2togtbl, purl to last 3 sts, P2tog, P1 [24 sts].

Next row: K4, K2tog, ssK, K8, ssK, K2tog, K4 [20 sts].

Next row: P3, P2tog, P2togtbl, P6, P2togtbl, P2tog, P3 [16 sts].

Next row: K2, K2tog, ssK, K4, ssK, K2tog, K2 [12 sts].

Cast off rem sts on WS.

Ears (make two)

Using white yarn and 2.75mm (UK 12, US 2) needles, cast on 8 sts.

Work 2 rows in SS.

Next row: K1, K2tog, K2, ssK, K1 [6 sts].

Purl 1 row.

Next row: K1, K2tog, ssK, K1 [4 sts].

Purl 1 row.

Next row: K2tog, ssK [2 sts].

Next row: P2tog.

Fasten off rem st.

Ear linings (make two)

Using pink yarn and 2mm (UK 14, US 0) needles, cast on 7 sts.

Work 2 rows in SS.

Next row: K1, K2tog, K1, ssK, K1 [5 sts].

Purl 1 row.

Next row: K2tog, K1, ssK [3 sts].

Purl 1 row.

Next row: sl1, K2tog, psso [1 st].

Fasten off rem st.

Nose

Using pink yarn and 2mm (UK 14, US 0) needles, cast on 3 sts.

Work 2 rows in SS.

Next row: sl1, K2tog, psso [1 st].

Fasten off rem st.

Back leg (right)

**Using white yarn and 2.75mm (UK 12, US 2) needles, cast on 6 sts and knit 1 row.

Next row: P1, M1, purl to last st, M1, P1 [8 sts].

Next row: K1, M1, knit to last st, M1, K1 [10 sts].

Starting with a purl row, work 7 rows in SS**.

Next row: cast off 4 sts, K1, M1, knit to last st, M1, K1 [8 sts].

Next row: P1, M1, purl to last st, M1, P1 [10 sts].

Next row: K1, M1, knit to last st, M1, K1 [12 sts].

Next row: P1, M1, purl to last st, M1, P1 [14 sts].

Work 4 rows in SS.

Row 1: K1, ssK, knit to last 3 sts, K2tog, K1 [12 sts].

Row 2: purl

Rep rows 1 and 2 once more and then row 1 once more [8 sts].

Next row: P1, P2togtbl, purl to last 3 sts, P2tog, P1 [6 sts].

Cast off rem sts.

Back leg (left)

Follow instructions for right back leg from ** to **.

Knit 1 row.

Next row: cast off 4 sts, P1, M1, purl to last st, M1, P1 [8 sts].

Next row: K1, M1, knit to last st, M1, K1 [10 sts].

Next row: P1, M1, purl to last st, M1, P1 [12 sts].

Next row: K1, M1, knit to last st, M1, K1 [14 sts].

Work 4 rows in SS.

Row 1: (WS) P1, P2togtbl, purl to last 3 sts, P2tog, P1 [12 sts].

Row 2: knit.

Rep rows 1 and 2 once more and then row 1 once more [8 sts].

Next row: K1, K2tog, knit to last 3 sts, ssK, K1 [6 sts].

Cast off rem sts.

Making up

Sew the side seams of the front legs. Stuff the front legs with toy filling. Fold the narrow middle front section of the cat downwards. Sew the edge of the middle section to the cast-off edge down towards the front legs. Continue sewing under the legs to the side of the body then towards the tail, stuffing with toy filling as you go. Sew the cast-on stitches of the front legs to the front of the body, using the picture as guidance.

Sew the tail seam, sliding a piece of chenille stick in as you go. Sew the base of the tail to the body.

Attach the safety eyes to the head and sew the back seam of the head. Stuff with toy filling. With WS together, sew an ear lining to each ear using pink yarn. Sew the ears to the top of the head. Using pink yarn, sew the nose in place and thread strong sewing thread through on either side of the nose to make whiskers. Sew the head to the body.

Sew the lower part of each back leg together and stuff gently. Pin the back legs in place, with the lower leg pointing downwards. Fold the lower leg up to lay along the side seam of the body. Use the picture as guidance. Sew in place, stitching the inside of the lower leg to the side of the body.

I only want to play!

Floppy Moggy

Throw him over your shoulder, cradle him in your arms or even dangle him upside down, this gorgeous moggy won't wriggle, scratch or even let out a plaintive miaow! He looks and feels just like the real thing, making him the ideal pet for even the most heavy-handed youngster.

Materials

Black fur yarn, 4 x 100g (4oz) balls
Two 18mm glass eyes
Pink 4-ply (fingering) yarn
Toy filling
Black sewing thread

Needles

2.75mm (UK 12, US 2) and 9mm (UK 00, US 13) knitting needles

Tension

3 sts to 2.5cm (1in) measured over GS using 9mm (UK 00, US 13) needles

Size

Approximately 40cm (16in) long, from tip of tail to front paws

Body

Made in one piece from bottom back edge (see diagram on page 83).
Using black fur yarn and 9mm (UK 00, US 13) needles, cast on 30 sts and knit 1 row.
*Next row: K1, M1, knit to last st, M1 [32 sts].
Knit 1 row.
Next row: K2tog, knit to last 2 sts, K2tog [30 sts].
Knit 1 row*.
Cast off 8 sts at beg of next 2 rows [14 sts].
Work 11cm (4¼in) in GS from cast-off edge.
Cast on 8 sts at beg of next 2 rows [30 sts].
Knit 1 row.
Work from * to * to shape the front legs.
Next row: K1, M1, K9, M1, K3, M1, K4, M1, K3, M1, K9, M1, K1 [36 sts].
Knit 1 row.
Next row: K2tog, knit to last 2 sts, K2tog [34 sts].
Knit 1 row*.
Cast off 8 sts at beg of next 2 rows [18 sts].
Work 11cm (4¼in) in GS from cast-off edge (back of body).
Next row: cast on 8 sts, K10, (K1, K2tog) twice, K1, (K1, K2tog) twice, knit to end of row [22 sts].
Cast on 8 sts at beg of next row [30 sts].

Pick me up and cuddle me — you'll never want to put me down!

Knit 1 row.

Work from * to * once more.

Cast off 13 sts at beg of next 2 rows [4 sts].

Cast on 2 sts at beg of next 2 rows [8 sts].

Continue in GS until tail measures 20cm (7¾in).

Next row: (K2tog) 4 times [4 sts].

Knit 1 row.

Thread yarn through rem sts and fasten off.

Head

Using black fur yarn and 9mm (UK 00, US 13) needles, cast on 12 sts.

Shape as follows:

Row 1: K2, (Kfb) twice, K4, (Kfb) twice, K2 [16 sts].

Row 2: K3, (Kfb) twice, K6, (Kfb) twice, K3 [20 sts].

Row 3: K4, (Kfb) twice, K8, (Kfb) twice, K4 [24 sts].

Row 4: K5, (Kfb) twice, K10, (Kfb) twice, K5 [28 sts].

Row 5: K6, (Kfb) twice, K12, (Kfb) twice, K6 [32 sts].

Work 4 rows in GS.

Row 10: K6, (K2tog) twice, K12, (K2tog) twice, K6 [28 sts].

Row 11: K5, (K2tog) twice, K10, (K2tog) twice, K5 [24 sts].

Row 12: K4, (K2tog) twice, K8, (K2tog) twice, K4 [20 sts].

Row 13: K3, (K2tog) twice, K6, (K2tog) twice, K3 [16 sts].

Row 14: K2, (K2tog) twice, K4, (K2tog) twice, K2 [12 sts].

Cast off.

Ears (make two)

Using black fur yarn and 9mm (UK 00, US 13) needles, cast on 7 sts and knit 2 rows.

Next row: K2tog, knit to last 2 sts, K2tog [5 sts].

Knit 1 row.

Rep last 2 rows once more [3 sts].

Next row: sl1, K2tog, psso.

Fasten off rem st.

Ear linings (make two)

Using pink yarn and 2.75mm (UK 12, US 2) needles, cast on 14 sts and work 2 rows in SS.

Next row: K1, K2tog, knit to last 3 sts, ssK, K1 [12 sts].

Purl 1 row.

Rep last 2 rows 4 more times [4 sts].

Next row: K2tog, ssK [2 sts].

Next row: P2tog [1 st].

Fasten off rem st.

Nose

Using pink yarn and 2.75mm (UK 12, US 2) needles, cast on 6 sts and work 2 rows in SS.

Next row: K1, K2tog, ssK, K1 [4 sts].

Next row: P1, P2tog, P1.

Next row: sl1, K2tog, psso [1 st].

Fasten off rem st.

Pads (make four)

Using pink yarn and 2.75mm (UK 12, US 2) needles, cast on 5 sts and knit 1 row.

Next row: P1, M1, purl to last st, M1, P1 [7 sts].

Knit 1 row.

Next row: P2tog, cast off 1 st, purl to end of row [5 sts].

Next row: K2tog, cast off 1 st, knit to end of row [3 sts].

Work 3 rows in SS.

Next row: sl1, K2tog, psso [1 st].

Fasten off rem st.

Toes (make twelve)

Using pink yarn and 2.75mm (UK 12, US 2) needles, cast on 3 sts and purl 1 row.

Next row: (K1, M1) twice, K1 [5 sts].

Starting with a purl row, work 3 rows in SS.

Next row: K2tog, K1, K2tog [3 sts].

Knit 1 row.

Cast off on WS.

Making up

There is no right or wrong side to this cat. Using the diagram on the facing page as guidance, fold over the cat's body as follows:

Bring one set of back legs over to the second set of back legs, folding the front legs in half in the process. Pin in place.

NB: if the pins slip out when you pin your cat together, try using safety pins instead.

Using a double length of black sewing thread, carefully sew up one side of the body and around the back leg. Try not to trap the cat's 'fur' under the black cotton as you sew.

Stuff gently.

Repeat the above instructions to sew the second side together. Lightly stuff the body before stitching the tail together and fastening it to the back of the cat's body at the start of the cast-on tail stitches. Do not stuff the tail.

Pin the back seam of the head together and sew using a double strand of black sewing cotton as before, keeping the fluffy part of the yarn away from the black thread as much as possible. Stuff quite firmly and then position the eyes before closing the end of the head.

Using the picture as guidance, pin and sew the nose in place using pink yarn. Also using pink yarn, sew the ear linings to the inside of the ears. Pin the ears to the top of the head, using the picture as guidance, and sew them in place using black sewing thread. Curve the bottom of each ear as you sew it on to give a good shape.

Lay the body out on a flat surface and place the head at the front of the body between the front paws. Stitch the head in place with a double strand of black thread.

Add pads and toes to the paws, sewing with pink yarn and using the main picture as guidance.

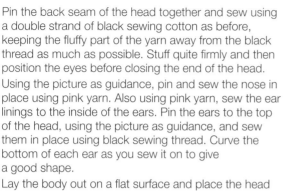

Doorstop Cat

Cats can be useful, and this one proves it! Big, heavy and full of character, he makes a wonderful doorstop (though he sometimes dreams of escaping and playing in the garden).

Body back

Use light brown for the body of the cat and dark brown for the markings. Make two mini balls of dark brown and use one each side. Using the intarsia technique (see page 13), twist the yarns together where they join to avoid holes.

Cast on 35 sts using light brown and 4mm (UK 8, US 6) needles. Knit 1 row.

Row 2: P1, M1, purl to last st, M1, P1 [37 sts].
Row 3: K1, M1, knit to last st, M1, K1 [39 sts].
Row 4: P1, M1, purl to last st, M1, P1 [41 sts].
Row 5: K40, M1, K1 [42 sts].

From now onwards, all sts in **bold** are worked in dark brown and all rem sts in light brown.

Row 6: **P6**, P35, M1, P1 [43 sts].
Row 7: **K5**, K30, **K8**.
Row 8: **P10**, P26, **P7**.
Row 9: **K8**, K24, **K11**.
Row 10: **P12**, P22, **P9**.
Row 11: **K10**, K23, **K10**.
Row 12: **P6**, P26, **P11**.
Row 13: **K12**, K27, **K4** [43 sts].
Row 14: **P2**, P28, **P13**.
Row 15: **K8**, K34, **K1**.
Row 16: P38, **P5**.
Row 17: **K3**, K36, **K4**.
Row 18: **P8**, P33, **P2**.
Row 19: K33, **K10**.
Row 20: **P13**, P26, **P4** [43 sts].
Row 21: **K7**, K25, **K11**.
Row 22: **P9**, P25, **P9**.
Row 23: **K10**, K26, **K7**.
Row 24: **P5**, P27, **P11**.
Row 25: **K12**, K27, **K4**.
Row 26: **P2**, P34, **P7**.
Row 27: **K5**, K23, **K3**, K11, **K1**.
Row 28: P9, **P5**, P25, **P4**.
Row 29: **K2**, K28, **K8**, K5 [43 sts].
Row 30: P3, **P9**, P31.
Row 31: **K3**, K29, **K10**, K1.
Row 32: **P1**, **P2togtbl**, **P7**, P26, **P7** [42 sts].
Row 33: **K10**, K24, **K8**.
Row 34: **P7**, P24, **P11**.
Row 35: **K8**, K17, **K3**, K7, **K4**, **K2tog**, **K1** [41 sts].
Row 36: **P5**, P6, **P4**, P20, **P6**.
Row 37: **K4**, K22, **K6**, K5, **K1**, **K2tog**, **K1** [40 sts].
Row 38: **P1**, P2togtbl, P4, **P6**, P24, **P3** [39 sts].
Row 39: **K1**, K2tog, K24, **K8**, K1, K2tog, **K1** [37 sts].
Row 40: **cast off 2 st**, **P8**, P26 [35 sts].
Row 41: **K5**, K22, **K5**, **K2tog**, **K1** [34 sts].
Row 42: **cast off 2 sts**, **P4**, P20, **P7** [32 sts].
Row 43: **K1**, **K2tog**, **K5**, K12, **K5**, K3, **K1**, **K2tog**, **K1** [30 sts].

Materials

Light brown 8-ply (DK) yarn
Dark brown 8-ply (DK) yarn
Black 4-ply (fingering) yarn
Two 12mm plastic safety eyes, painted on the backs with gold nail polish
Toy filling
Sock
Rice (to weight the doorstop)

Needles

2.75mm (UK 12, US 2) and 4mm (UK 8, US 6) knitting needles

Tension

5–6 sts to 2.5cm (1in) measured over SS using 4mm (UK 8, US 6) needles

Size

Approximately 23cm (9in) tall to top of head

Row 44: cast off 2 sts, P2, **P7**, P10, **P8** [28 sts].
Row 45: **K6**, K13, **K6**, K2tog, K1 [27 sts].
Row 46: **P1**, **P2tog**, **P4**, P16, **P4** [26 sts].
Row 47: **K3**, K17, **K3**, **K2tog**, **K1** [25 sts].
Row 48: **P1**, **P2tog**, **P1**, P19, **P2** [24 sts].
Row 49: **K1**, K21, **K2** [24 sts].
Row 50: **P1**, P23.
Row 51: **K1**, K20, K2tog, K1 [23 sts].
Row 52: **P3**, P17, **P3**.
Row 53: **K5**, K13, **K5**.
Row 54: **P4**, P13, **P6**.
Row 55: **K4**, K16, **K3**.
Row 56: **P2**, P19, **P2**.
Row 57: **K1**, K10, **K1**, K10, **K1**.
Row 58: P11, **P1**, P11.
Row 59: K8, **K1**, K1, **K3**, K1, **K1**, K8 [23 sts].
Row 60: P8, **P1**, P1, **P3**, P1, **P1**, P8.
Row 61: K7, **cast off 9 sts**, K6.

Row 62: turn and, working over first set of 7 sts, P7.
Row 63: K1, K2tog, K4 [6 sts].
Row 64: P6.
Row 65: K1, K2tog, K3 [5 sts].
Row 66: P5.
Row 67: K1, K2tog, K2 [4 sts].
Row 68: P2tog, P2togtbl.
Row 69: K2tog and fasten off rem st.
With WS facing, rejoin yarn to rem 7 sts.
Purl 1 row.
Next row: K4, K2togtbl, K1 [6 sts].
Next row: purl.
Next row: K3, K2togtbl, K1 [5 sts].
Next row: purl.
Next row: K2, K2togtbl, K1 [4 sts].
Next row: P2tog, P2togtbl [2 sts].
Next row: K2tog and fasten off rem st.

Body front

Using light brown, cast on 36 sts using 4mm (UK 8, US 6) needles and knit 1 row.

Row 2: P1, M1, P34, M1, P1 [38 sts].

Row 3: K1, M1, K36, M1, K1 [40 sts].

Row 4: P39, M1, P1 [41 sts].

Row 5: **K5**, K35, M1, K1 [42 sts].

Row 6: **P1**, **M1**, **P3**, P31, **P7** [43 sts].

Row 7: **K9**, K27, **K7**.

Row 8: **P8**, P24, **P11**.

Row 9: **K12**, K22, **K9**.

Row 10: **P10**, P23, **P10**.

Row 11: **K6**, K26, **K11**.

Row 12: **P12**, P27, **K4** [43 sts].

Row 13: **K2**, K28, **K13**.

Row 14: **P8**, P34, **P1**.

Row 15: K38, **K5**.

Row 16: **P3**, P36, **P4**.

Row 17: **K8**, K33, **K2**.

Row 18: P33, **P10**.

Row 19: **K13**, K26, **K4**.

Row 20: **P7**, P35, **P11**.

Row 21: **K9**, K25, **K9** [43 sts].

Row 22: **P10**, P26, **P7**.

Row 23: **K5**, K27, **K11**.

Row 24: **P12**, P27, **P4**.

Row 25: **K2**, K34, **K7**.

Row 26: **P7**, P34, **P2**.

Row 27: **K1**, K11, **K3**, K23, **K5**.

Row 28: **P4**, P25, **P5**, P9.

Row 29: K5, **K8**, K28, **K2** [43 sts].

Row 30: P31, **P9**, P3.

Row 31: **K11**, K29, **K3**.

Row 32: **P7**, P26, **P7**, **P2togtbl**, **P1** [42 sts].

Row 33: **K8**, K24, **K10**.

Row 34: **P11**, P24, **P7**.

Row 35: **K1**, **K2tog**, **K4**, K7, **K3**, K17, **K8** [41 sts].

Row 36: **P6**, P20, **P4**, P6, **P5**.

Row 37: **K1**, k2tog, **K1**, K5, **K6**, K22, **K4** [40 sts].

Row 38: **P3**, P24, **P6**, P4, P2togtbl, **P1** [39 sts].

Row 39: cast off 2 sts, K2, **K8**, K25, **K1** [37 sts].

Row 40: P27, **P7**, **P2togtbl**, P1 [36 sts].

Row 41: cast off 2 sts, **K2tog**, **K4**, K22, **K5** [33 sts].

Row 42: **P7**, P22, **P4**.

Row 43: **cast off 2 sts**, **K2**, K3, **K5**, K13, **K7** [31 sts].

Row 44: **P8**, P10, **P7**, P3, **P2togtbl**, **P1** [30 sts].

Row 45: **cast off 2 sts**, **K6**, K14, **K4**, **K2tog**, **K1** [27 sts].

Row 46: **P4**, P17, **P6**.

Row 47: **K1**, **K2tog**, **K3**, K18, **K3** [26 sts].

Row 48: **P2**, P20, **P1**, **P2togtbl**, **P1** [25 sts].

Row 49: **K1**, **K2tog**, K21, **K1** [24 sts].

Row 50: P23, **P1**.

Row 51: K1, K2tog, K20, **K1** [23 sts].

Row 52: **P3**, P17, **P3**.

Row 53: **K5**, K13, **K5**.

Row 54: **P6**, P13, **P4**.

Row 55: **K4**, K16, **K3**.

Row 56: **P2**, P19, **P2**.

Row 57: **K1**, K10, **K1**, K10, **K1**.

Row 58: P11, **P1**, P11.

Row 59: K8, **K1**, K1, **K3**, K1, **K1**, K8.

Row 60: P8, **P1**, P1, **P3**, P1, **P1**, P8.

Row 61: K7, **cast off 10 sts**, K7.

Turn and, working over first set of 7 sts, P7.

Next row: knit.

Next row: P4, P2togtbl, P1.

Next row: knit.

Next row: P3, P2togtbl, P1.
Next row: knit.
Next row: P2, P2togtbl, P1.
Next row: K2tog twice.
Next row: P2tog and fasten off rem st.
With WS facing, rejoin yarn to rem 7 sts and purl 1 row.
Next row: knit.
Next row: P1, P2tog, P2.
Next row: knit.
Next row: P1, P2tog, P3.
Next row: knit.
Next row: P1, P2togtbl, P2.
Next row: K2tog, twice [4 sts].
Next row: P2tog and fasten off.

Base
Using light brown and 4mm (UK 8, US 6) knitting needles, cast on 18 sts and work 2 rows in SS.
Next row: K1, M1, knit to last st, M1, K1 [20 sts].
Next row: P1, M1, purl to last st, M1, P1 [22 sts].
Rep last 2 rows twice more [30 sts].
Work 4 rows in SS.
Next row: K1, K2tog, knit to last 3 sts, ssK, K1 [28 sts].
Next row: P1, P2togtbl, purl to last 3 sts, P2tog, P1 [26 sts].
Rep last 2 rows twice more [18 sts].
Work 2 rows in SS.
Cast off.

Tail
Using dark brown and 4mm (UK 8, US 6) knitting needles, cast on 10 sts and work 11cm (4¼in) in SS, ending with a RS row.
*Next row: P4, w&t.
K4, turn.
P6, w&t.
K6, turn.
P8, w&t.
K8, turn.
Rep from * a further 4 times.
Purl 1 row.
Next row: K1, K2tog, knit to last 3 sts, ssK, K1 [8 sts].
Purl 1 row.
Rep last 2 rows twice more [4 sts].
Cast off.

Nose
Using black 4-ply (fingering) yarn and 2.75mm (UK 12, US 2) knitting needles, cast on 4 sts and knit 1 row.
Next row: (P2tog) twice [2 sts].
Next row: K2tog.
Fasten off rem st.

Feet (make two)
Using light brown and 4mm (UK 8, US 6) knitting needles, cast on 2 sts.
Row 1: (Kfb) twice [4 sts].
Row 2: (Kfb) 4 times [8 sts].
Row 3: knit.
Row 4: (P2tog) 4 times [4 sts].
Row 5: (K2tog) twice [2 sts].
Row 6: purl.
Rep these 5 rows twice more to make 3 toes. Cast off rem 2 sts.

Making up
Sew the side seams of the cat, matching the markings on the front and the back. Attach the eyes and stuff two-thirds of the cat with toy filling. Half fill the sock with rice so that it fits inside the cat. Sew across the sock just above the rice, and fold the top part of the sock back over the stuffed part. Place the sock inside the cat and pad the cat with toy filling until you are happy with the shape. Pin and sew the base in place. Pin and sew the tail in place using the picture as guidance, and stuff gently to make it look three dimensional. Sew the nose in place and embroider the mouth and whiskers using the picture as guidance.
Gather the edges of each foot to give the toes definition and sew them to the seam between the base of the cat and the body, using the picture for guidance.

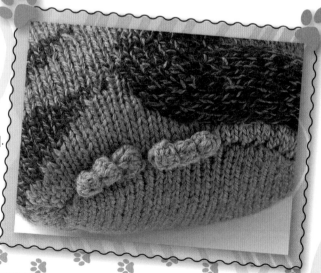

Alley Cat

This artful alley cat is full of mischief, but he's just a big softy at heart.
With his cheeky grin and gentle nature, you will find him irresistible!

Materials

Ginger 8-ply (DK) yarn
Cream 8-ply (DK) yarn
Black 4-ply (fingering) yarn
Weighting beads
Toy filling
Two 12mm plastic safety eyes, painted on the backs with gold nail polish

Needles

2.5mm (UK 13, US 1) and 4mm (UK 8, US 6) knitting needles

Tension

5 sts to 2.5cm (1in) measured over SS using 4mm (UK 8, US 6) needles

Size

Approximately 31cm (12¼in) tall, from paws to top of head

When knitting with the ginger yarn you are working in reverse SS, which means the 'wrong' side of the work becomes the 'right' side. This gives texture to the cat. When working with the cream yarn, you are working in SS. So for the front, back and head, work in SS and then use the 'wrong' side of the knitting as the front of the work.

Front

Using ginger yarn and 4mm (UK 8, US 6) needles, cast on 20 sts and work 2 rows in SS.
Row 1: K1, M1, knit to last st, M1, K1 [22 sts].
Row 2: P1, M1, purl to last st, M1, P1 [24 sts].
Rep last 2 rows 3 more times [36 sts].
Next row: K26, w&t.
P16, w&t.
K19, w&t.
P22, w&t.
Knit to end of row.
Starting with a purl row, work 5 rows in SS.
Next row: K1, K2tog, knit to last 3 sts, ssK, K1 [34 sts].

Work 3 rows in SS.
Rep last 4 rows 7 times [20 sts].
Next row: K1, K2tog, knit to last 3 sts, ssK, K1 [18 sts].
Purl 1 row.
Rep last 2 rows twice more [14 sts].
Cast off.

Back

Using ginger yarn and 4mm (UK 8, US 6) needles, cast on 20 sts and work 2 rows in SS.
Row 1: K1, K2tog, knit to last 3 sts, ssK, K1 [18 sts].
Row 2: purl 1 row.
Rep last 2 rows 4 more times [10 sts].
Next row: K10, pick up 7 sts purlwise and purl these sts [17 sts].
Next row: P17, pick up 7 sts knitwise and knit these sts [24 sts].
Row 1: K1, M1, knit to last st, M1, K1 [26 sts].
Row 2: P1, M1, purl to last st, M1, P1 [28 sts].
Rep last 2 rows 3 more times [40 sts].
Work 6 rows in SS.
Next row: K1, K2tog, knit to last 3 sts, ssK, K1 [38 sts].
Work 3 rows in SS.
Rep last 4 rows once more [36 sts].
Next row: K1, K2tog, K14, K2tog, K14, ssK, K1 [33 sts].
Work 3 rows in SS.
Next row: K1, K2tog, K12, K2tog, K12, ssK, K1 [30 sts].
Work 3 rows in SS.
Next row: K1, K2tog, K11, K2tog, K11, ssK, K1 [27 sts].
Work 3 rows in SS.
Next row: K1, K2tog, K9, K2tog, K10, ssK, K1 [24 sts].
Work 3 rows in SS.
Next row: K1, K2tog, knit to last 3 sts, ssK, K1 [22 sts].
Work 3 rows in SS.
Rep last 4 rows once more [20 sts].
Next row: K1, K2tog, knit to last 3 sts, ssK, K1 [18 sts].
Purl 1 row.
Rep last 2 rows twice more [14 sts].
Cast off.

Bib

Using cream yarn and 4mm (UK 8, US 6) needles, cast on 12 sts and knit 1 row.
Row 1: P1, M1, purl to last st, M1, P1 [14 sts].
Row 2: K1, M1, knit to last st, M1, K1 [16 sts].
Rep last 2 rows once more [20 sts].
Rep row 1 once more [22 sts].
Work 5 rows in SS.
Next row: K1, k2tog, knit to last 3 sts, ssK, K1 [20 sts].
Work 3 rows in SS.
Rep last 4 rows 6 more times [8 sts].
Cast off.

Head

The head is worked in one piece.
Using ginger yarn and 4mm (UK 8, US 6) needles, cast on 16 sts and work 2 rows in SS.
***Row 1:** K1, M1, knit to last st, M1, K1 [18 sts].
Row 2: P1, M1, purl to last st, M1, P1 [20 sts].
Rep last 2 rows once more [24 sts].
Rep row 1 once more [26 sts].
Work 13 rows in SS*.
Row 1: K1, K2tog, knit to last 3 sts, ssK, K1 [24 sts].
Row 2: P1, P2togtbl, purl to last 3 sts, P2tog, P1 [14 sts].
Rep row 1 once more [12 sts].
Purl 1 row.
Rep from * to * [26 sts].
Row 1: K1, K2tog, knit to last 3 sts, ssK, K1 [24 sts].
Row 2: P1, P2togtbl, purl to last 3 sts, P2tog, P1 [22 sts].
Rep last 2 rows once more [18 sts].
Rep row 1 once more [16 sts].
Cast off.

Face

Using cream yarn and 4mm (UK 8, US 6) needles, cast on 18 sts.
Row 1: K1, M1, K7, M1, K2, M1, K7, M1, K1 [22 sts].
Purl 1 row.
Next row: K1, K2tog, K7, M1, K2, M1, K7, ssK, K1 [22 sts].
Purl 1 row.
Rep last 2 rows 4 more times.
Next row: K1, K2tog, knit to last 3 sts, ssK, K1 [20 sts].
Purl 1 row.

Nose
Using black 4-ply (fingering) yarn and 2.5mm (UK 13, US 1) knitting needles, cast on 5 sts.
Work 2 rows in SS.
Next row: K2tog, K1, ssK [3 sts].
Purl 1 row.
Next row: sl1, K2tog, psso.
Thread yarn through rem st and tighten.

Arms (make two)
Using ginger yarn and 4mm (UK 8, US 6) needles, cast on 18 sts and work 7cm (2¾in) in rev SS, ending with a WS row (knit row).
Next row: change to cream and, starting with a knit row, work 4 rows in SS.
Next row: K1, M1, K7, M1, K2, M1, K7, M1, K1 [22 sts].
Purl 1 row.
Next row: K1, M1, K9, M1, K2, M1, K9, M1, K1 [26 sts].
Purl 1 row.
Work 2 rows in SS.
Next row: K1, K2tog, K7, ssK, K2, K2tog, K7, ssK, K1 [22 sts].
Next row: P1, P2tog, P5, P2togtbl, P2, P2tog, P5, P2togtbl, P1 [18 sts].
Cast off.

Legs (make two)
Using ginger yarn and 4mm (UK 8, US 6) needles, cast on 18 sts and work 8cm (3¼in) in rev SS.
Cast off.

Feet (make two)
Using cream yarn and 4mm (UK 8, US 6) needles, cast on 7 sts and knit 1 row.
Next row: P1, M1, purl to last st, M1, P1 [9 sts].
Next row: K1, M1, knit to last st, M1, K1 [11 sts].
Work 5 rows in SS.
Row 1: K1, M1, knit to last st, M1, K1 [13 sts].
Row 2: purl 1 row.
Rep last 2 rows once more [15 sts].
Work 2 rows in SS.
Next row: K1, K2tog, knit to last 3 sts, ssK, K1 [13 sts].
Next row: P1, P2togtbl, purl to last 3 sts, P2tog, P1 [11 sts].
Work 3 rows in SS.
Next row: P1, M1, purl to last st, M1, P1 [13 sts].
Next row: K1, M1, knit to last st, M1, K1 [15 sts].

Next row: K1, K2tog, K4, K2tog, K2, ssK, K4, ssK, K1 [16 sts].
Purl 1 row.
Next row: K1, K2tog, K2, K2tog, K2, ssK, K2, ssK, K1 [12 sts].
Purl 1 row.
Next row: K1, K2tog, knit to last 3 sts, ssK, K1 [10 sts].
Purl 1 row.
Rep last 2 rows 3 more times [4 sts].
Next row: K2tog, ssK [2 sts].
Cast off.

Ears (make two)
The ears are worked in GS.
Cast on 12 sts using ginger yarn and 4mm (UK 8, US 6) needles, and knit 2 rows.
Next row: K1, K2tog, knit to last 3 sts, ssK, K1 [10 sts].
Knit 2 rows.
Rep last 3 rows 3 more times [4 sts].
Next row: K2tog, ssK.
K2tog.
Thread yarn through rem st.

Work 2 rows in SS.

Row 1: K1, K2tog, knit to last 3 sts, ssK, K1 [13 sts].

Row 2: purl.

Rep last 2 rows once more [11 sts].

Work 4 rows in SS.

Next row: K1, K2tog, knit to last 3 sts, ssK, K1 [9 sts].

Next row: P1, P2togtbl, purl to last 3 sts, P2tog, P1 [7 sts].

Cast off.

Tail

Using ginger yarn and 4mm (UK 8, US 6) needles, cast on 16 sts and work 14cm (5½in) in rev SS, ending with a WS row. Change to cream and, starting with a RS row (knit), continue in SS for 8 rows.

Next row: (K2, K2tog) 4 times [12 sts].

Purl 1 row.

Next row: (K2, K2tog) 3 times [9 sts].

Purl 1 row.

Next row: (K2tog) 4 times, K1 [5 sts].

Thread yarn through rem sts and tighten.

Making up

Sew the seam on each arm (remembering that the back of the ginger knitting is the right side), stuff and oversew the end of the arm with cream yarn to form a paw shape, using the picture for guidance. Sew each leg seam, again with the back of the knitting on the right side. Sew the foot seams and oversew to make paws, as for the arms. Sew the bottom of each leg to the top of a foot, placing weighting beads in the bottom of the leg and filling the rest of the leg with toy filling.

Sew the side seam of the tail, placing weighting beads at the end of the tail and filling the rest with toy filling.

Position the arms and legs, placing them in the seams of the body. Sew the seams, stitching the arms and legs in place as you go. Place weighting beads in the bottom of the body and fill the rest with toy filling. Sew the tail to the back of the body, using the picture for guidance.

With the back of the knitting facing outwards, sew the side seams of the head. Stuff lightly with toy filling and sew the face to the front of the head with the RS facing outwards, stuffing gently to give definition as you sew.

Attach the safety eyes and place more toy filling inside the head. Sew the nose to the front of the face and embroider the mouth and whiskers with black yarn. Sew the ears to the top of the head, using the picture as guidance. Sew the head to the body.

Sew the bib to the front of the body, matching the top of the bib to the cream edge of the face.

Christmas Cat

What a lovely surprise to find in your Christmas stocking! This cute kitten makes a great tree decoration or stocking filler for the festive season. The pattern for the little white mouse is also provided.

Materials

Red 5-ply (sportweight) yarn
Green 5-ply (sportweight) yarn
Grey 8-ply (DK) yarn
Pale pink 2-ply (laceweight) yarn
White 4-ply (fingering) Angora yarn
8mm plastic safety eyes, painted on the backs with gold nail polish
Toy filling
Two tiny beads
Black strong sewing cotton
White sewing cotton

Needles

2.75mm (UK 12, US 2) and 3.25mm (UK 10, US 3) knitting needles
Sewing needle

Tension

6 sts to 2.5cm (1in) measured over GS using 5-ply (sportweight) yarn and 3.25mm (UK 10, US 3) needles

Size

Approximately 20cm (7¾in) long, from top of cat's head to stocking toe

Happy Christmas!

The heel and toe of the Christmas stocking are knitted in GS using short row shaping. Start by working one less stitch on each row to create the heel/toe shape. Once you have reached the middle of the heel/toe, work outwards again, working one extra stitch on every row to get back to the top of the heel/toe. The heel and toe are worked over half the row (17 sts).

Stocking

Using red yarn and 3.25mm (UK 10, US 3) needles, cast on a picot edging as follows:
(Cast on 5 sts, cast off 2 sts) 11 times, cast on 1 st [34 sts].
Work 12 rows in GS.
Work 4 rows in SS.
Change to green yarn and work 2 rows in SS.
Change to red yarn and work 2 rows in SS.
Rep the last 4 rows a further 6 times.
Work 2 rows in green.
Knit 1 row in red.
Begin heel shaping:
NB: all slipped stitches are slipped knitwise.
*Next row: (WS) K17, turn.
Next row: sl1, K15, turn.
Next row: sl1, K14, turn.
Next row: sl1, K13, turn.
Next row: sl1, K12, turn.
Next row: sl1, K11, turn.
Next row: sl1, K10, turn.
Next row: sl1, K9, turn.
Next row: sl1, K8, turn.
Next row: sl1, K7, turn.
Next row: sl1, K6, turn.
Next row: sl1, K5, turn.
Next row: sl1, K4, turn.
Next row: sl1, K3, turn.
You will now start working outwards again, working one extra stitch on each row.

Next row: sl1, K4, turn.
Next row: sl1, K5, turn.
Next row: sl1, K6, turn.
Next row: sl1, K7, turn.
Next row: sl1, K8, turn.
Next row: sl1, K9, turn.
Next row: sl1, K10, turn.
Next row: sl1, K11, turn.
Next row: sl1, K12, turn.
Next row: sl1, K13, turn.
Next row: sl1, K14, turn.
Next row: sl1, K15, turn.
Next row: sl1, K16, turn.
Next row: sl1, K17, turn. *
Next row: purl across all sts [34 sts].
Change to green and work 2 rows in SS.
Work 2 rows in red.
Rep the last 4 rows 3 more times.
Work 2 rows in green.
Next row: knit 1 row in red.
Work from * to * as for heel shaping.

With RS together, cast off rem 34 sts using three-needle cast-off method and red yarn (see page 12).

Head
Using grey yarn and 3.25mm (UK 10, US 3) needles, cast on 12 sts.
Next row: K1, M1, K5, M1, K5, M1, K1 [15 sts].
Purl 1 row.
Next row: K6, M1, K3, M1, K6 [17 sts].
Next row: P1, M1, P6, M1, P3, M1, P6, M1, P1 [21 sts].
Next row: K9, M1, K3, M1, K9 [23 sts].
Next row: P1, M1, P9, M1, P3, M1, P9, M1, P1 [27 sts].
Next row: K12, M1, K3, M1, K12 [29 sts].
Starting with a purl row, work 3 rows in SS.
Next row: K11, K2tog, K3, ssK, K11 [27 sts].
Next row: P10, P2togtbl, P3, P2tog, P10 [25 sts].
Next row: K9, K2tog, K3, ssK, K9 [23 sts].
Next row: P8, P2togtbl, P3, P2tog, P8 [21 sts].
Next row: K7, K2tog, K3, ssK, K7 [19 sts].
Next row: P6, P2togtbl, P3, P2tog, P6 [17 sts].
Next row: K1, K2tog, K11, ssK, K1 [15 sts].
Next row: P1, P2togtbl, purl to last 3 sts, P2tog, P1 [13 sts].
Cast off 3 sts, K6, cast off rem 3 sts.
With WS facing, rejoin yarn to rem 7 sts and work 11 rows in SS, starting with a purl row.
Next row: K1, K2tog, K1, ssK, K1 [5 sts].
Starting with a purl row, work 3 rows in SS.
Next row: K1, sl1, K2tog, psso, K1 [3 sts].
Purl 1 row.
Cast off.

Ears (make two)
Using grey yarn and 3.25mm (UK 10, US 3) needles, cast on 6 sts and work 2 rows in SS.
Next row: K2tog, K2, ssK [4 sts].
Purl 1 row.
Next row: K2tog, ssK [2 sts].
Next row: P2tog.
Fasten off rem st.

Ear linings (make two)
Using a double strand of pink 2-ply (laceweight) yarn and 2.75mm (UK 12, US 2) needles, cast on 7 sts and work 2 rows in SS.
Next row: K2tog, knit to last 2 sts, ssK [5 sts].
Purl 1 row.
Rep the last 2 rows once more [3 sts].
Next row: sl1, K2tog, psso.
Fasten off rem st.

Nose

Using a double strand of pink 2-ply laceweight yarn and 2.75mm (UK 12, US 2) needles, cast on 3 sts.
Work 2 rows in SS.
Next row: sl1, K2tog, psso [1 st].
Fasten off rem st.

Feet (make two)

Using grey yarn and 3.25mm (UK 10, US 3) knitting needles, cast on 2 sts.
Row 1: (Kfb) twice [4 sts].
Row 2: (Kfb) 4 times [8 sts].
Row 3: knit.
Row 4: (P2tog) 4 times [4 sts].
Row 5: (K2tog) twice [2 sts].
Row 6: purl.
Rep these 5 rows twice more to make 3 toes. Cast off rem 2 sts.

Mouse body

Using white Angora and 2.75mm (UK 12, US 2) needles, cast on 3 sts and knit 1 row.
Next row: K1, M1, knit to last st, M1, K1 [5 sts].
Rep this row 6 more times [17 sts].
Next row: (K2tog) 4 times, K1, (K2tog) 4 times [9 sts].
Next row: (K2tog) twice, K1, (K2tog) twice [5 sts].
Thread yarn through rem sts and fasten off.

Mouse ears (make two)

Using white Angora and 2.75mm (UK 12, US 2) needles, cast on 4 sts and knit 4 rows.
Next row: (K2tog) twice [2 sts].
Next row: K2tog.
Fasten off rem st.

Mouse tail

Using white Angora and 2.75mm (UK 12, US 2) needles, cast on 3 sts and work in SS until tail measures 4cm (1½in). Thread yarn through sts to fasten off. Alternatively, work the mouse's tail as an i-cord to save sewing it up (see page 12).

Hanging loop

Using red yarn and 3.25mm (UK 10, US 3) needles, cast on 18 sts and knit 1 row.
Cast off.

Making up

Join the side seam of the stocking, carefully lining up the stripes. Fold over the red cuff at the top of the stocking and gently stuff the stocking with toy filling. Attach the safety eyes to the cat's head and sew

the gusset into place. Stuff with toy filling. With WS together, sew an ear lining to an ear and repeat for the second ear. Sew the ears to the top of the cat's head, using the picture as guidance. Sew the nose in place. Thread some whiskers through using black sewing cotton. Using a needle and thread, sew from the base of the head through to the back of each eye, pull the thread back down to the base and tighten. This gives a fantastic shape to the head. Fold the hanging loop in half and sew it to the side seam on the inside of the stocking.

Place the cat's head inside the stocking and sew the head to the inside edge of the stocking all the way round, so that the head is peeping out of the stocking.

Sew around each of the cat's 'toes' and gather to form them into a bobble. Stitch the two feet to the front of the stocking just under head, where the head and the stocking meet.

Sew the seam of the mouse's body and stuff it with toy filling. Sew the mouse's ears in place, using the picture as guidance. Using white sewing thread and a sewing needle, sew the tiny beads (eyes) to the head and make the whiskers. Using pink yarn, embroider the nose. Sew the tail to the base of the body. Sew the mouse to the stocking.

Happy Family

This mother and her two playful kittens make a delightful family group. Knit as many kittens as you like and in whatever colours you choose – a gorgeous gift for cat lovers everywhere! The instructions for the cat basket are provided on page 108.

Mother cat

Materials
White 10-ply (Aran) yarn
Black 10-ply (Aran) yarn
Pale pink 4-ply (fingering) yarn
Red 4-ply (fingering) yarn
Toy filling
Chenille sticks
Two 10mm glass eyes
Black embroidery thread
10mm brass bell

Needles
2.75mm (UK 12, US 2) and 4mm (UK 8, US 6) knitting needles
Stitch markers
Darning needle

Tension
4 sts to 2.5cm (1in) measured over SS using 4mm (UK 8, US 6) needles

Size
Approximately 15cm (6in) tall from front paws to top of head

Body (and front legs)
Using white yarn and 4mm (UK 8, US 6) needles, cast on 10 sts.
Starting at right front foot:
Knit 1 row.
Next row: P8, turn.
K3, turn, P3, turn, K3, turn.

P5 (to end of row).

Next row: K2, K3B, K5.

Work 5 rows in SS.

Next row: K6, M1, K3, M1, K1 [12 sts].

Purl 1 row.

Change to black yarn and work 3 rows in SS.

Cast off 1 st at beg of next row (WS) [11 sts].

Cast off 5 sts at beg of next row [6 sts].

Cast on 8 sts at beg of next row [14 sts].

Next row: K1, M1, knit to last st, M1, K1 [16 sts].

P1, M1, purl to end of row [17 sts].

Next row: knit to last st, M1, K1 [18 sts].

P1, M1, purl to end of row [19 sts].

Work 24 rows in SS, placing marker at beg and end of row 12.

Next row: knit to last 3 sts, K2tog, K1 [18 sts].

Next row: P1, P2tog, purl to end of row [17 sts].

Next row: K1, ssK, knit to last 3 sts, K2tog, K1 [15 sts].

Next row: cast off 8 sts, P3, P2tog, P1 [6 sts].

Next row: (RS) cast on 5 sts at beg of row, knit to end of row [11 sts].

Next row: cast on 1 st at beg of row, purl to end of row [12 sts].

Starting with a knit row, work 3 rows in SS.

Change to white yarn.

Starting with a purl row, work 3 rows in SS.

Next row: K5, K2tog, K2, ssK, K1 [10 sts].

Starting with a purl row, work 5 rows in SS.

Next row: K5, turn.

P3, turn.

K3, turn.

P3, turn.

K8 (to end of row).

Next row: P5, P3B, P2.

Cast off rem 10 sts.

Belly

Using white yarn and 4mm (UK 8, US 6) needles, cast on 3 sts and work 2 rows in SS.

Next row: K1, M1, knit to last st, M1, K1 [5 sts].

Work 3 rows in SS.

Rep the last 4 rows 3 more times [11 sts].

Work 14 rows in SS.

Next row: K1, K2tog, knit to last 3 sts, ssK, K1 [9 sts].

Work 3 rows in SS.

Rep the last 4 rows once more [7 sts].

Next row: K2tog, K3, ssK [5 sts].

Purl 1 row.

Cast off.

Let's play cat and mouse!

Head

Using black yarn and 4mm (UK 8, US 6) needles, cast on 12 sts.

Next row: K1, M1, K5, M1, K5, M1, K1 [15 sts].

Purl 1 row.

Using the Fair Isle technique, work as follows (see page 12). Work all sts in **bold** in black and all other sts in white.

Next row: **K6**, **M1**, K3, **M1**, **K6** [17 sts].

Next row: **P1**, **M1**, **P6**, M1, P3, M1, **P6**, **M1**, **P1** [21 sts].

Next row: **K8**, K1, M1, K3, M1, K1, **K8** [23 sts].

Next row: **P1**, **M1**, **P7**, P2, M1, P3, M1, P2, **P7**, **M1**, **P1** [27 sts].

Next row: **K9**, K3, M1, K3, M1, K3, **K9** [29 sts].

Next row: **P9**, P11, **P9**.

Next row: **K9**, K11, **K9**.

Next row: **P9**, P11, **P9**.

Next row: **K9**, K2, K2tog, K3, ssK, K2, **K9** [27 sts].

Next row: **P9**, P1, P2togtbl, P3, P2tog, P1, **P9** [25 sts].

Next row: **K9**, K2tog, K3, ssK, **K9** [23 sts].

Next row: **P8**, **P2tog**, P3, **P2togtbl**, **P8** [21 sts].

Next row: **K7**, **K2tog**, K3, **ssK**, **K7** [19 sts].

Next row: **P6**, **P2tog**, P3, **P2togtbl**, **P6** [17 sts].

Next row: **K1**, **K2tog**, **K5**, K1, **K5**, **ssK**, **K1** [15 sts].

This is the last row that uses white yarn. From now on use just black yarn.

Next row: P1, P2togtbl, purl to last 3 sts, P2tog, P1 [13 sts].

Cast off 3 sts, K6, cast off rem 3 sts.

With RS facing, rejoin yarn to rem 7 sts and work 12 rows in SS.

Next row: K1, K2tog, K1, ssK, K1 [5 sts].

Work 3 rows in SS.

Next row: K1, sl1, K2tog, psso, K1 [3 sts].

Purl 1 row.

Cast off.

Back leg (left)

Using white yarn and 4mm (UK 8, US 6) needles, cast on 10 sts and knit 1 row.

Next row: P5, turn.

K3, turn.

P3, turn.

K3, turn.

P8 (to end of row).

Next row: K5, K3B, K2.

Work 7 rows in SS.

Next row: K4, w&t.

P3, w&t.

K3, w&t.

P3, w&t.

K3, w&t.

P4 (to end of row).

Next row: (K1, M1) twice, K3, M1, K1, M1, K4 [14 sts].

P8, join in black yarn, P6 in black.

From now on work all sts in **bold** using black yarn.

Next row: **K2**, **M1**, **K1**, **M1**, **K4**, K1, M1, K1, M1, K5 [18 sts].

Next row: P8, **P10**.

Next row: **cast off 3 sts**, **M1**, **K7**, K6, M1, K1 [17 sts].

Next row: cast off 6 sts, M1, **purl to last st**, **M1**, **K1** [13 sts].

Change to black yarn and work 4 rows in SS.

Next row: K1, K2tog, knit to last 3 sts, ssK, K1 [11 sts].

Next row: P1, P2togtbl, purl to last 3 sts, P2tog, P1 [9 sts].

Rep last 2 rows once more [5 sts].

Cast off rem 5 sts.

Back leg (right)

Using white yarn and 4mm (UK 8, US 6) needles, cast on 10 sts and knit 1 row.

Next row: P8, turn.

K3, turn.

P3, turn.

K3, turn.

P5 (to end of row).

Next row: K2, K3B, K5.

Work 7 rows in SS.

Next row: K9, w&t.

P3, w&t.

K3, w&t.

P3, w&t.

K3, w&t.

P9 (to end of row).

Next row: K4, M1, K1, M1, K3, (M1, K1) twice [14 sts].

Join in black yarn and from now on work all sts in **bold** in black yarn.

Next row: **P6**, P8.

Next row: K5, M1, K1, M1, K1, **K4**, **M1**, **K1**, **M1**, **K2** [18 sts].

Next row: **P10**, P8.

Next row: cast off 6 sts, M1, **knit to last st, M1, K1** [14 sts].

Next row: cast off 3 sts, M1, purl to last st, M1, P1 [13 sts].

Change to black yarn and work 4 rows in SS.

Next row: K1, K2tog, knit to last 3 sts, ssK, K1 [11 sts].

Next row: P1, P2togtbl, purl to last 3 sts, P2tog, P1 [9 sts].

Rep last 2 rows once more [5 sts].

Cast off rem 5 sts.

Tail

Using black yarn and 4mm (UK 8, US 6) needles, cast on 7 sts and work 8cm (3¼in) in SS, ending with a WS row.

Change to white yarn and work 2 rows in SS.

Next row: (K1, K2tog) twice, K1 [5 sts].

Work 1 row in SS.

Thread yarn through sts and fasten off.

Ears (make two)

Using black yarn and 4mm (UK 8, US 6) needles, cast on 7 sts and work 2 rows in SS.

Next row: K1, K2tog, K1, SSK, K1. [5 sts].

P 1 row.

Next row: K2tog, K1, SSK. [3 sts].

P 1 row.

Next row: Sl1, K2tog, psso.

Fasten off rem st.

Ear linings (make two)

Repeat ear instructions above using pale pink 4-ply (fingering) yarn and 2.75mm (UK 12, US 2) knitting needles.

Nose

Cast on 4 sts using pink 4-ply (fingering) yarn and 2.75mm (UK 12, US 2) knitting needles.

Work 2 rows in SS.

Next row: K2tog, ssK [2 sts].

Next row: P2tog.

Fasten off rem st.

Collar

Using red yarn cast on 5 sts and work in SS until collar is long enough to go around the cat's neck. Cast off.

Making up

Starting with the body, gather the cast-on/cast-off end of one of the front paws into a circle by running a thread through the stitches. Sew the side seam of the leg, insert a chenille stick and stuff gently. Repeat for the second leg. Match the middle of the cast-off end of the cat's belly with the marker at the tail end of the body, and match the middle of the cast-on edge with the marker between the front paws. Sew the belly evenly down the sides of the body, leaving a small opening for stuffing. Be careful not to pucker the front legs when catching the black stitches to the belly. Do not sew the top of the leg opening to the belly at this point. Stuff with toy filling and sew closed.

Stuff and sew the top of each front leg to the belly. Sew the foot and leg seam of each back leg as for the front legs and sew them to the body, inserting a chenille stick and stuffing gently, using the picture as guidance. Sew the side seam of the tail. Insert a chenille stick down the tail and sew it to the back of the body as shown in the pictures.

Using the pictures as a guide, fix the eyes to the head. Fold the head piece in half and sew the back-gusset seams. Leave the neck edge open and stuff gently. Using a darning needle and yarn, sew from the base of the head to the back of each eye, pull the yarn back down to the base and tighten. This gives a good shape to the head.

With WS together, sew the ear and ear linings together for each ear. Use the picture to position and sew the ears to the head. Using pink yarn, sew the nose in place. Embroider on the mouth and whiskers using black embroidery thread.

Place the collar around the cat's neck and carefully sew the ends together. Sew the bell in place.

Kitten

Body (and front legs)

Using white yarn cast on 8 sts.
Starting at right front foot:
Knit 1 row.
Next row: P6, turn.
K3, turn.
P3, turn.
K3, turn.
P5 (to end of row).
Next row: K2, K3B, K3.
Work 5 rows in SS.
Next row: K4, M1, K3, M1, K1 [10 sts].
Purl 1 row.
Change to black yarn and knit 1 row.
Cast off 1 st at beg of next row (WS)
[9 sts].
Cast off 4 sts at beg of next row [5 sts].
Cast on 8 sts at beg of next row [13 sts].
Next row: K1, M1, knit to last st, M1, K1
[15 sts].

P1, M1, purl to end of row [16 sts].
Next row: knit to last st, M1, K1 [17 sts].
Purl 1 row.
Work 16 rows in SS, placing marker at beg
and end of row 8.
Next row: knit to last 3 sts, ssK, K1 [16 sts].
P1, P2tog, purl to end of row [15 sts].
Next row: K1, K2tog, knit to last 3 sts, ssK,
K1 [13 sts].
Cast off 8 sts at beg of next row [5 sts].
Cast on 4 sts at beg of foll row [9 sts].
Cast on 1 st at beg of next row [10 sts].
Change to white yarn and work 2 rows in SS.
Next row: K4, K2tog, K1, ssK, K1 [8 sts].
Work 6 rows in SS.
Next row: P6, turn.
K3, turn.
P3, turn.
K3, turn.
P5 (to end of row).
Next row: K2, K3B, K3.
Cast off rem 8 sts.

Belly

Using white yarn, cast on 3 sts and work 2 rows in SS.

Next row: K1, M1, knit to last st, M1, K1 [5 sts].

Work 3 rows in SS.

Rep last 4 rows twice more [9 sts].

Work 10 rows in SS.

Next row: K1, K2tog, knit to last 3 sts, ssK, K1 [7 sts].

Work 3 rows in SS.

Rep last 4 rows once more [5 sts].

Next row: K2tog, K1, ssK [3 sts].

Purl 1 row. Cast off.

Head

Using black yarn, cast on 8 sts.

K1, M1, K3, M1, K3, M1, K1 [11 sts].

Purl 1 row.

Using the Fair Isle technique, work as follows (see page 12). Work all sts in **bold** in black and all other sts in white.

Next row: **K4**, **M1**, K3, **M1**, **K4** [13 sts].

Next row: **P1**, **M1**, **P4**, M1, P3, M1, **P4**, **M1**, **P1** [17 sts].

Next row: **K6**, K1, M1, K3, M1, K1, **K6** [19 sts].

Next row: **P1**, **M1**, **P5**, P2, M1, P3, M1, P2, **P5**, **M1**, **P1** [23 sts].

Next row: **K7**, K3, M1, K3, M1, K3, **K7** [25 sts].

Next row: **P7**, P11, **P7**.

Next row: **K7**, K2, K2tog, K3, ssK, K2, **K7** [23 sts].

Next row: **P7**, P1, P2togtbl, P3, P2tog, P1, **P7** [21 sts].

Next row: **K7**, K2tog, K3, ssK, **K7** [19 sts].

Next row: **P6**, **P2tog**, P3, **P2togtbl**, **P6** [17 sts].

Next row: **K5**, **K2tog**, K3, **ssK**, **K5** [15 sts].

Next row: **P4**, **P2tog**, **P1**, P1, **P1**, **P2togtbl**, **P4** [13 sts]. This is the last row that uses white yarn. From now on use just black yarn.

Next row: K1, K2tog, K7, ssK, K1 [11 sts].

Next row: P1, P2togtbl, purl to last 3 sts, P2tog, P1 [9 sts].

Cast off 2 sts, K4, cast off rem 2 sts.

With RS facing, rejoin yarn to rem 5 sts and work 6 rows in SS.

Next row: K1, M1, knit to last st, M1, K1 [7 sts].

Work 3 rows in SS.

Next row: K1, K2tog, K1, ssK, K1 [5 sts].

Work 7 rows in SS.

Next row: K2tog, K1, ssK [3 sts].

Purl 1 row. Cast off.

Back leg (left)

Using white yarn, cast on 8 sts and knit 1 row.

Next row: P5, turn.

K3, turn, P3, turn, K3, turn.

P6 (to end of row).

Next row: K3, K3B, K2.

Work 5 rows in SS.

Next row: K3, w&t.

P2, w&t.

K2, w&t.

P3 (to end of row).

Next row: (K1, M1) twice, K2, M1, K1, M1, K3 [12 sts].

Purl 1 row.

Next row: K2, M1, K1, M1, K4, M1, K1, M1, K4 [16 sts].

P8 sts in white yarn, join in black yarn, P8 in black.

From now on work all sts in **bold** using black yarn and all other sts in white yarn.

Next row: **cast off 3 sts**, **M1**, **K5**, K6, M1, K1 [15 sts].

Next row: cast off 5 sts, M1, P1, **P7**, **M1**, **K1** [12 sts].

Change to black yarn and work 4 rows in SS.

Next row: K1, K2tog, knit to last 3 sts, ssK, K1 [10 sts].

Next row: P1, P2togtbl, purl to last 3 sts, P2tog, P1 [8 sts].

Rep last 2 rows once more [4 sts].

Cast off rem 4 sts.

Back leg (right)

Using white yarn, cast on 8 sts and knit 1 row.

Next row: P6, turn.

K3, turn.

P3, turn.

K3, turn.

P5 (to end of row).

Next row: K2, K3B, K3.

Work 5 rows in SS.

Next row: K7, w&t.

P2, w&t.

K2, w&t.

P7 (to end of row).

Next row: K3, M1, K1, M1, K2, (M1, K1) twice [12 sts].

Purl 1 row.

Next row: K4, M1, K1, M1, K4, M1, K1, M1, K2 [16 sts].

Join in black yarn, P8, P8 in white.

From now on work all sts in **bold** in black yarn.

Next row: cast off 5 sts, M1, K1, **K8**, **M1**, **K1** [13 sts].

Next row: cast off 3 sts, **M1**, **P8**, M1, K1 [12 sts].

Change to black yarn and work 4 rows in SS.

Next row: K1, K2tog, knit to last 3 sts, ssK, K1 [10 sts].

Next row: P1, P2togtbl, purl to last 3 sts, P2tog, P1 [8 sts].

Rep last 2 rows once more [4 sts].

Cast off rem 4 sts.

Tail

Using black yarn, cast on 7 sts and work 4.5cm (1¾in) in SS.

Change to white yarn and work 3 rows in SS.

Next row: (K1, K2tog) twice, K1 [5 sts].

Work 1 row in SS.

Thread yarn through sts and fasten off.

Ears (make two)

Using black yarn, cast on 5 sts and work 2 rows in SS.

Next row: K2tog, K1, ssK [3 sts].

Purl 1 row.

Next row: sl1, K2tog, psso [1 st].

Fasten off rem st.

Ear linings (make two)

Using pale pink yarn, cast on 4 sts and work 2 rows in SS.

Next row: K1, K2tog, K1 [3 sts].

Purl 1 row.

Next row: sl1, K2tog, psso [1 st].

Fasten off rem st.

Collar

Using red yarn, cast on 3 sts and work in SS until collar is long enough to go around the kitten's neck. Cast off.

Making up

Starting with the body, gather the cast-on/cast-off end of each front paw into a circle by running a thread through the stitches. Sew the side seam of each front leg, insert a chenille stick and stuff gently. Match the middle of the cast-off end of the cat's belly with the marker at the tail end of the body, and the middle of the cast-on edge to the marker between the front paws. Sew the belly evenly down the sides of body, leaving a small opening for stuffing. Be careful not to pucker the front legs when catching the sts to the belly. Do not sew the top of the leg opening to the belly at this point. Stuff with toy filling and sew closed.

Stuff and sew the top of each front leg to the belly. Sew the foot and leg seams of the back legs as for the front legs and sew the back legs to the body, inserting a chenille stick and stuffing gently. Use the pictures as guidance. Sew the side seam of the tail. Insert a chenille stick down the tail and sew the tail to the back of the body as shown in the pictures.

Using the pictures as a guide, fix the eyes to the head. Fold the head piece in half and sew the back-gusset seams, gently stuffing as you close, leaving the neck edge open. Using a darning needle and yarn, sew from the base of the head to the back of each eye, pull the yarn back down to the base and tighten. This gives the head a good shape. With WS together, sew the ear linings to the ears and sew the ears to the head, using the picture for placement. Using pale pink yarn, embroider the nose. Using black embroidery thread, embroider the mouth and whiskers.

Place the collar around the kitten's neck and carefully sew the ends together. Sew the bell in place.

Scratching Post

Every cat needs something to sharpen its claws on, even a knitted one! This handy scratching post also has a colourful dangly bird for your kittens to play with.

Materials

Brown 10-ply (Aran) yarn
Beige 10-ply (Aran) yarn
4-ply (fingering) colour-changing yarn, or oddments of single-colour 4-ply (fingering) yarn
Cardboard
Empty kitchen-roll tube
Rice (to weight the post)
Small amount of toy filling
Yellow embroidery thread
Black embroidery thread

Needles

2.5mm (UK 13, US 1) and 4mm (UK 8, US 6) knitting needles

Tension

4–5 sts to 2.5cm (1in) measured over GS using 10-ply (Aran) yarn

Size

Approximately 13cm (5in) tall

Base (make two)

Using 4mm (UK 8, US 6) needles and brown yarn, cast on 20 sts and work in GS until piece is square. Cast off.

Top (make two)

Using 4mm (UK 8, US 6) needles and brown yarn, cast on 12 sts and work in GS until piece is square. Cast off.

Post

Using 4mm (UK 8, US 6) needles and beige yarn, cast on 20 sts and work in GS until work measures 10cm (4in). Cast off.

Bird's body

Using 4-ply yarn and 2.5mm (UK 13, US 1) needles, cast on 4 sts and purl 1 row.
Next row: K1, M1, K2, M1, K1 [6 sts].
Purl 1 row.
Next row: K2, M1, K2, M1, K2 [8 sts].
Purl 1 row.
Next row: K3, M1, K2, M1, K3 [10 sts].
Next row: P4, M1, P2, M1, P4 [12 sts].
Next row: K5, M1, K2, M1, K5 [14 sts].
Next row: P6, M1, P2, M1, P6 [16 sts].
Work 2 rows in SS.
Next row: K5, K2tog, K2, ssK, K5 [14 sts].
Next row: P4, P2tog, P2, P2togtbl, P4 [12 sts].
Next row: K3, K2tog, K2, ssK, K3 [10 sts].
Next row: P2, P2tog, P2, P2togtbl, P2 [8 sts].
Next row: K1, K2tog, K2, ssK, K1 [6 sts].
Purl 1 row.
Next row: K1, M1, knit to last st, M1, K1 [8 sts].
Work 2 rows in SS.
Next row: (P2tog) 4 times [4 sts].
Cast off.

Bird's wings (make two)

Using 4-ply yarn and 2.5mm (UK 13, US 1) needles, cast on 2 sts.
Next row: K1, M1, K1 [3 sts].
Purl 1 row.
Next row: K1, M1, K2 [4 sts].
Purl 1 row.

Next row: K1, K2tog, K1 [3 sts].
Purl 1 row.
Next row: sl1, K2tog, psso.
Fasten off rem st.

Making up

Cut a piece of card to fit inside the two knitted base sections. Repeat with the top of the scratching post. Sew the edges together with the card inside.

Cut a 10cm (4in) length of kitchen-roll tube to fit inside the post. Make a cut down the side of the tube.

Fold the knitting around the tube, making the tube narrower, if necessary, to fit. Sew the side seam of the post around the tube. Sew the post to the base, fill the tube with rice to weight it and sew the top in place.

Sew the seam of the bird, stuffing as you go. Sew the wings in place and sew 'loops' to make a tail. Embroider the beak using yellow embroidery thread and the eyes using black embroidery thread. Fix the bird to a corner of the scratching post with a length of beige yarn.

Cat Bed

Cats lead such a busy life, it's only fair they should have a comfortable bed to sleep in too. This one fits the bill perfectly.

Materials
Beige 10-ply (Aran) yarn

Needles
4mm (UK 8, US 6) knitting needles
Stitch holder

Tension
4–5 sts to 2.5cm (1in), measured over GS

Size
Approximately 4cm (1½in) deep and 11cm (4¼in) deep

Work in GS throughout.

Base
Cast on 10 sts and knit 1 row.
Next row: K1, M1, knit to last st, M1, K1 [12 sts].
Rep last row 7 more times [26 sts].
Knit 12 rows.
Next row: K1, K2tog, knit to last 3 sts, K2tog, K1 [24 sts].
Rep last row 7 more times [10 sts].
Cast off.

Sides
Cast on 16 sts. Work in GS until bed fits approximately half way around the base.
Next row: K6, cast off 4 sts, K5 (leaving 2 sets of 6 sts).
Continue over first set of 6 sts. Place second set of 6 sts on a holder.
*Knit 1 row.

Next row: K1, K2tog, knit to end of row [5 sts].
Work 3 rows in GS.
Rep last 4 rows once more [4 sts].
Next row: K1, M1, knit to end of row [5 sts].
Work 3 rows in GS.
Rep last 4 rows once more [6 sts]*.
With WS facing, rejoin yarn to 6 sts on holder and work from * to * to match first side.
Next row: K6, cast on 4 sts, K6 [16 sts].
Continue in GS until edge of bed fits around the base.

Making up
Fold the top part of the bed in half along its length and sew the decreased edges together. This will be the top edge of the bed. Sew the two side edges of the knitting to the outside edge of the base, as shown in the picture. Sew the back seam.

Balls

Materials
Blue, red and yellow 5-ply (sportweight) yarn

Needles
3.25mm (UK 10, US 3) knitting needles

Tension
Not relevant.

Size
Approximately 5.5cm (2¼in), 4.5cm (1¾in) and 3cm (1¼in) diameter

These colourful balls make perfect playthings for your cats and kittens.

To make the balls smaller or larger, use thinner or thicker yarn and vary the knitting needles accordingly.

Small ball
Using yellow yarn, cast on 14 sts and purl 1 row.
Work increase rows as follows:
K1, (Kfb, K1, Kfb) to last st, K1. Purl 1 row [22 sts].
K1, (Kfb, K3, Kfb) to last st, K1. Purl 1 row [30 sts].
Work 2 rows in SS. Work decrease rows as follows:
K1, (K2tog, K3, ssK) to last st, K1. Purl 1 row [22 sts].
K1, (K2tog, K1, ssK) to last st, K1. Purl 1 row [14 sts].
Thread yarn through rem sts and fasten off.

Medium ball
Using red yarn, cast on 14 sts and purl 1 row.
Work increase rows as follows:
K1, (Kfb, K1, Kfb) to last st, K1. Purl 1 row [22 sts].
K1, (Kfb, K3, Kfb) to last st, K1. Purl 1 row [30 sts].
K1, (Kfb, K5, Kfb) to last st, K1. Purl 1 row [38 sts].
K1, (Kfb, K7, Kfb) to last st, K1. Purl 1 row [46 sts].
Work 4 rows in SS. Work decrease rows as follows:
K1, (K2tog, K7, ssK) to last st, K1. Purl 1 row [38 sts].
K1, (K2tog, K5, ssK) to last st, K1. Purl 1 row [30 sts].
K1, (K2tog, K3, ssK) to last st, K1. Purl 1 row [22 sts].
K1, (K2tog, K1, ssK) to last st, K1. Purl 1 row [14 sts].
Thread yarn through rem sts and fasten off.

Large ball
Using blue yarn, cast on 14 sts and purl 1 row.
Work increase rows as follows:
K1, (Kfb, K1, Kfb) to last st, K1. Purl 1 row [22 sts].
K1, (Kfb, K3, Kfb) to last st, K1. Purl 1 row [30 sts].
K1, (Kfb, K5, Kfb) to last st, K1. Purl 1 row [38 sts].
K1, (Kfb, K7, Kfb) to last st, K1. Purl 1 row [46 sts].
K1, (Kfb, K9, Kfb) to last st, K1. Purl 1 row [54 sts].
K1, (Kfb, K11, Kfb) to last st, K1. Purl 1 row [62 sts].
Work 6 rows in SS. Work decrease rows as follows:
K1, (K2tog, K11, ssk) to last st, K1. Purl 1 row [54 sts].
K1, (K2tog, K9, ssK) to last st, K1. Purl 1 row [46 sts].
K1, (K2tog, K7, ssK) to last st, K1. Purl 1 row [38 sts].
K1, (K2tog, K5, ssK) to last st, K1. Purl 1 row [30 sts].
K1, (K2tog, K3, ssK) to last st, K1. Purl 1 row [22 sts].
K1, (K2tog, K1, ssK) to last st, K1. Purl 1 row [14 sts].
Thread yarn through rem sts and fasten off.

Making up
Sew the side seam and stuff firmly. Gather the cast-on edge and pull together. Sew closed.

Mice

A cat's life simply wouldn't be complete without the odd mouse to chase, so here are a few knitted ones that you can make for your little woolly felines. If you prefer, work the tails of the mice as i-cords (see page 12) to avoid having a seam to sew up.

Materials
Grey 2-ply (laceweight) yarn (used double throughout)
Toy filling
Small amount of pink 2-ply (laceweight) yarn or embroidery thread
Small black beads

Needles
2.75mm (UK 12, US 2) knitting needles
Sewing needle

Tension
Not relevant

Size
Approximately 5cm (2in), 4cm (1½in) and 2.5cm (1in) long, excluding tail

Small mouse

Body
Using a double strand of grey 2-ply (laceweight) yarn and 2.75mm (UK 12, US 2) needles, cast on 3 sts and knit 1 row.
Next row: K1, M1, knit to last st, M1, K1 [5 sts].
Rep this row 6 more times [17 sts].
Next row: (K2tog) 4 times, K1, (K2tog) 4 times [9 sts].
Next row: (K2tog) twice, K1, (K2tog) twice [5 sts].
Thread yarn through rem sts and fasten off.

Ears (make two)
Using a double strand of grey 2-ply (laceweight) yarn and 2.75mm (UK 12, US 2) needles, cast on 4 sts and knit 2 rows.
Next row: (K2tog) twice [2 sts].
Next row: K2tog.
Fasten off rem st.

Tail
Using a double strand of grey 2-ply (laceweight) yarn and 2.75mm (UK 12, US 2) needles, cast on 3 sts and work in SS until tail measures 2cm (¾in). Thread the yarn through the sts to fasten off.

Medium mouse

Body

Using a double strand of grey 2-ply (laceweight) yarn and 2.75mm (UK 12, US 2) needles, cast on 3 sts and knit 1 row.

Next row: K1, M1, knit to last st, M1, K1 [5 sts].

Rep this row 8 more times [21 sts].

Next row: (K2tog) 5 times, K1, (K2tog) 5 times [11 sts].

Next row: (K2tog) twice, sl1, K2tog, psso, (K2tog) twice [5 sts].

Thread yarn through rem sts and fasten off.

Ears (make two)

Using a double strand of grey 2-ply (laceweight) yarn and 2.75mm (UK 12, US 2) needles, cast on 4 sts and knit 4 rows.

Next row: (K2tog) twice [2 sts].

Next row: K2tog.

Fasten off rem st.

Tail

Using a double strand of grey 2-ply (laceweight) yarn and 2.75mm (UK 12, US 2) needles, cast on 4 sts and work in SS until tail measures 3cm (1¼in). Thread the yarn through the sts to fasten off.

Large mouse

Body

Using a double strand of grey 2-ply (laceweight) yarn and 2.75mm (UK 12, US 2) needles, cast on 3 sts and knit 1 row.

Next row: K1, M1, knit to last st, M1, K1 [5 sts].

Rep this row 11 more times [27 sts].

Next row: (K2tog) 6 times, K1, (K2tog) 7 times [14 sts].

Next row: (K2tog) 7 times [7 sts].

Next row: K2tog, K1, (K2tog) twice [4 sts].

Thread yarn through rem sts and fasten off.

Ears (make two)

Using a double strand of grey 2-ply (laceweight) yarn and 2.75mm (UK 12, US 2) needles, cast on 5 sts and knit 4 rows.

Next row: K2tog, K1, K2tog [3 sts].

Next row: sl1, K2tog, psso.

Fasten off rem st.

Tail

Using a double strand of grey 2-ply (laceweight) yarn and 2.75mm (UK 12, US 2) needles, cast on 4 sts and work in SS until tail measures 4cm (1½in). Thread yarn through rem sts to fasten off.

Making up

Follow these instructions for each size of mouse.

Starting from the base of the mouse, sew the side seam, stuffing with toy filling as you go. Sew the ears to the front of the mouse, using the pictures for guidance. Using pink yarn (or embroidery thread), oversew a nose on the front of the mouse. Using a single strand of 2-ply (laceweight) yarn and a sewing needle, attach two beads above the nose for eyes. Sew the tail to the base of the mouse.

It's cosy in here! Just right for a cat nap.

Abbreviations

beg	beginning
cm	centimetres
foll	following
GS	garter stitch
in	inch
inc	increase
K	knit
K2tog	knit 2 stitches together
K3B	pass next stitch to RH needle, pick up stitch 3 rows below and knit together with this stitch. Repeat for next two stitches. This creates a 'fold' in the knitting.
Kfb	knit into front and back of stitch (increasing one stitch)
Kfbf	knit into the front, back and front of the stitch (increasing two stitches)
M	marker
M1	make a backwards loop on your needle by twisting the yarn towards you and slipping the resulting loop on to the right-hand needle. On the following row, knit or purl through the back of the stitch. This produces a very neat result
P	purl
P2tog	purl 2 stitches together

P3B	pass next stitch to RH needle, pick up stitch 3 rows below and purl together with this stitch. Repeat for next two stitches
PM	place marker
psso	pass slipped stitch over
rem	remaining
rep	repeat
rev	reverse
RH	right hand
RS	right side
sl	slip a stitch
SM	slip marker from left to right needle
SS	stocking stitch
ssK	slip 2 stitches knitwise one at a time, pass the 2 slipped stitches back to the left needle, knit both together through the back of the loop.
ssP	slip 2 stitches knitwise one at a time, pass the two slipped sts back to the left needle, purl 2 slipped stitches together from the back, left to right.
st(s)	stitch(es)
tbl	through the back of the loop
tog	together
w&t	wrap and turn (see techniques, page 12)
WS	wrong side
yo	yarn over needle

For a complete list of all our books see

www.searchpress.com

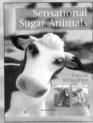

To request a free catalogue, go to http://www.searchpress.com/requestcat.asp